NOW HEAR THIS!

Listening Comprehension for High Beginners

and Intermediates

Barbara H. Foley

Institute for Intensive English
Union College, New Jersey

HEINLE & HEINLE PUBLISHERS
A Division of Wadsworth, Inc.
Boston, Massachusetts 02116

Library of Congress Cataloging in Publication Data

Foley, Barbara H.
  Now hear this!

  1. English language--Text-books for foreign speakers.
2. Listening.   3. Comprehension.   I. Title.
PE1128.F57   1984   428.3'4   83-22089
ISBN 0-8384-2993-9

Cover and interior book design by Diana Esterly

Illustrations by Marci Davis

Photographs courtesy of: Donna Jernigan—The Photo Source (pages 18, 36, 66, 72, 102); Australian Information Service (page 54); Massachusetts State Lottery Commission (page 96); U.S. Geological Survey, Department of the Interior (page 108); The Titanic Historical Society (page 114).

First printing: February 1984

Printed in the U.S.A.

14 15

INTRODUCTION

Now Hear This! is intended for high beginning and low intermediate students of English as a Second Language. It is a program for both listening comprehension and listening discrimination. Its purpose is to develop effective listening skills for high interest conversations, descriptions, and narrations.

The emphasis throughout the units is on listening in context. As they follow each topic, students hear the sound and flow of English. They hear the organization of the language and the sequence and relationship of ideas. They hear new vocabulary in a meaningful setting. As students concentrate on the message, the sense of the language becomes clearer to them.

Now Hear This! seeks to improve four listening skills: (1) determining vocabulary meaning from context; (2) identifying a main idea with supporting details; (3) listening for a specific purpose; and (4) recognizing specific grammatical structures within a setting.

The book contains twenty-two units, each with a different topic of interest to students. The suggested procedure is as follows:

Discussion

The photo or illustration accompanying each unit and the questions in this section introduce the unit topic to the class. These are used to provide a schema for the topic and to arouse the students' interest in the selection. At the outset teachers should encourage students to offer information, personal stories, and opinions. The focus here is on developing a background for listening to the passage.

Vocabulary

In listening to the story or dialog, students will encounter new vocabulary words. The vocabulary exercises before each selection lead students to determine meaning from the content.

Teachers should play the taped vocabulary words and ask the students to repeat each one. The teacher may want the students to listen to the words once or twice, first, then repeat.

LISTENING COMPREHENSION

A. **Fill in.**   The students will hear sentences which include the eight new vocabulary words. As they hear each sentence, they should write the correct vocabulary word in the blank, referring to the list for spelling. Teachers can stop the tape after each item if the students need additional writing time.

B. **Word association.**   Using the sentences above as the context, students do this exercise, circling the two words that can be associated with the new item.

C. **First listening.**   Students listen to the complete taped story once. The tape, or parts of it, may be played as many times as the class requests. Then, the students tell the class any information they remember about the story. The focus here is not on grammar, but on the comprehension of the story. One student may only be able to give back one small piece of information. Another may be able to remember several facts. Teachers should prompt students to recall most of the information. Students who may have had difficulty understanding the selection will learn from their classmates.

D. Second listening.   The second listening asks the class to listen to the taped story again, this time with a specific task in mind. Students may be asked to record figures, check attitudes, put events in sequence, number actions, and so forth.

E. Third listening.   The third listening is a true-false exercise. The students read the statements first, then they listen to the tape again, concentrating on any information they may need to determine if the statement is true or false.

F. Comprehension questions.   In this section the students listen to six questions and are asked to circle the correct answer.

LISTENING DISCRIMINATION

Throughout the unit so far, the concentration has been on content. Now, the concentration is on structure through listening discrimination exercises. Each unit focuses on a particular tense. Although there are a variety of tenses within each selection, one tense predominates. The students are now asked to consider its usage in several sentences from the taped story.

G. Listen and choose.   Students listen to ten sentences, circling the verb they hear. The class can check this exercise as a group by replaying the tape as the teacher asks the students which forms they hear. Students must hear the verb form before they can write it.

H. Listen and write.   Students listen to ten sentences, this time writing the verb they hear. Teachers can stop the tape after each item if students need additional writing time. The teacher should replay the tape and have the students check their answers.

I. Listen and decide.   The students hear ten sentences in the stated tense. They circle the words *correct* or *incorrect*, depending on what they hear. The students are listening to how the sentence sounds. As the class checks answers to this exercise, students may ask that a particular sentence be played several times. The last two units, which focus on tense contrast, do not contain this particular exercise because they do not concentrate on a specific tense.

J. Cloze.   If the selection is short, the cloze exercise is the entire story or dialog. If the selection is long, only sections of it are included. Only the verbs are omitted in this activity. The tape may be played again before the class begins this exercise. It is suggested that the students do the cloze exercise in small groups of three or four students, helping one another complete the blanks.

CONTENTS

NOW HEAR THIS!

APARTMENT PROBLEMS 1

Focus: **Present continuous tense**

Discussion: **Discuss these questions with your classmates.**

Do you own a house or do you rent a house or an apartment? How did you find your home? Did you look in the newspaper? Did a friend tell you about it?

Do you have (or did you ever have) any problems in your home? For example: the heat isn't working, the refrigerator isn't cold enough, etc. Describe the problem.

Vocabulary: **Repeat each word after the tape.**

are expecting
fix
stuck
is overflowing

few
mess
radiator
is leaking

LISTENING COMPREHENSION

A. Fill in.   Listen to these sentences. Fill in the new vocabulary words from the list above.

1. I can't open the door. It's _____ .

2. It's cold in this room. The _____ isn't turned on.

3. They don't have any children. They _____ their first child next month.

4. The pipe in the sink is stopped up. Water _____ onto the floor.

5. Our apartment is small, there are only a _____ rooms.

6. The refrigerator doesn't work. The landlord is going to _____ it.

1

7. There's a problem in the bathroom upstairs. The water is _____ through the ceiling into the living room.

8. Nothing is clean and food and clothes are all over. This place is a

    _____ .

B. Word association. Circle the two words that you can associate with each new vocabulary word.

1. fix   broken, repair, hot
2. stuck   won't open, hit, tight
3. expecting   good, baby, pregnant
4. mess   dirty, old, not in order
5. radiator   heat, winter, food
6. overflowing   water, going over, fly
7. few   many, not many, three or four
8. leaking   pipe, clean, water

C. First listening. Look at the picture and listen to the story. After you listen, tell the class any information you remember about the story.

D. Second listening. Listen to the story again. There are six problems in this apartment. List them below as you listen to the tape.

_____

_____

_____

_____

_____

_____

E. Third listening. Read these statements. Then, listen to the tape a third time. After you listen, write *T* if the statement is true; *F* if the statement is false.

_____ 1. Theresa and Charles are looking for a house.

_____ 2. Theresa is expecting a baby.

_____ 3. The family is showing Theresa and Charles their apartment.

_____ 4. There are only a few problems.

_____ 5. The apartment is clean.

_____ 6. Theresa can't open the refrigerator door.

_____ 7. The apartment is hot.

_____ 8. In the bathroom, there's a lot of water on the floor.

_____ 9. There are probably problems in other apartments in this building.

_____ 10. Theresa and Charles are going to rent this apartment.

F. Comprehension questions. Listen to each question. Circle the correct answer.

1. a. one
   b. two
   c. three
2. a. today
   b. next week
   c. in two months
3. a. It's a mess.
   b. It's stuck.
   c. It doesn't work.
4. a. Water is leaking from the ceiling.
   b. The light isn't working.
   c. It's nighttime.
5. a. The sink is overflowing.
   b. There's a problem in the apartment above this one.
   c. Charles can't turn the water off.
6. a. The family doesn't take care of the apartment.
   b. The landlord doesn't take care of the building.

LISTENING DISCRIMINATION

G. Listen and choose. Listen to each sentence. Circle the verb you hear.

1. a. expecting	b. is expecting	c. are expecting
2. a. looking	b. is looking	c. are looking
3. a. talking	b. is talking	c. are talking
4. a. living	b. is living	c. are living
5. a. smoking	b. is smoking	c. are smoking

6. a. not working   b. isn't working   c. aren't working
7. a. coming   b. is coming   c. are coming
8. a. overflowing   b. is overflowing   c. are overflowing
9. a. leaking   b. is leaking   c. are leaking
10. a. leaving   b. is leaving   c. are leaving

H. Listen and write.   Listen to each sentence. Write the verb you hear.

1. _____   6. _____

2. _____   7. _____

3. _____   8. _____

4. _____   9. _____

5. _____   10. _____

I. Listen and decide.   You will hear a statement in the present continuous tense. Is the grammar correct or incorrect? Circle *correct* or *incorrect*.

1. correct   incorrect   6. correct   incorrect
2. correct   incorrect   7. correct   incorrect
3. correct   incorrect   8. correct   incorrect
4. correct   incorrect   9. correct   incorrect
5. correct   incorrect   10. correct   incorrect

APARTMENT PROBLEMS

J. Cloze.   Fill in each blank with the correct word.

Theresa and Charles live in Chicago. They rent a one-bedroom apartment. Theresa

_____ _____ a baby in two months, so they _____

_____ for a larger apartment.

Theresa and Charles _____ _____ to the landlord in a large

apartment building. He _____ _____ them an apartment in his

building. A family _____ _____ there now, but they're going to move

next week. The landlord _____ also _____ that there are a few

problems in the apartment, but he's going to fix them.

Theresa and Charles _____ _____ around the apartment. They can't believe the mess! In the kitchen, the oven door _____ open and the oven _____ _____ . Theresa _____ _____ to open the refrigerator, but she can't. The door _____ stuck. And the heat _____ _____ , no hot air _____ _____ up from the radiator.

Charles _____ in the bathroom. He can't see too well because the light _____ _____ . The sink _____ _____ . Water _____ _____ all over the floor and Charles can't turn it off. And water _____ _____ from the ceiling. There's probably a problem in the apartment above this one.

Theresa and Charles aren't going to rent this apartment. They _____ _____ in a hurry!

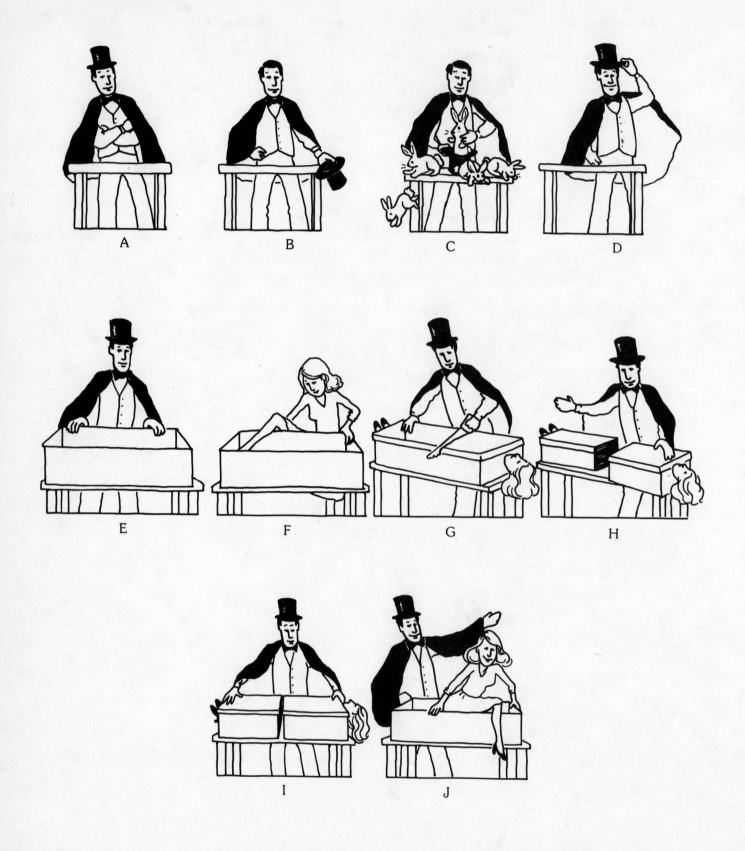

A

B

C

D

E

F

G

H

I

J

THE MAGICIAN 2

Focus: **Present continuous tense; prepositions of place**

Discussion: **Discuss these questions with your classmates.**

Did you ever watch a magician, in person or on tv? Can you describe any of the tricks you saw? Can you do any tricks?

Vocabulary: **Repeat each word after the tape.**

magician   volunteer
tricks   piece
audience   is climbing
stage   is sawing

LISTENING COMPREHENSION

A. Fill in. Listen to these sentences. Fill in the new vocabulary words from the list above.

1. The _____ is sitting in the theater and watching the magician.

2. The magician is standing on the _____ so that everyone can see him.

3. The man _____ the tree in half.

4. I don't understand how the magician can do those _____ .

5. The woman _____ into the large, empty box.

6. The _____ is wearing a tall black hat and a black coat.

7. It looks like the magician is sawing her in half, but she's really in one

   _____ .

8. The magician is asking for someone to help him. He needs a

   _____ .

B. Word association.
Circle the two words that you can associate with each new vocabulary word.

1. magician   trick, black hat, light
2. trick   fall, magician, cards
3. audience   watch, tree, theater
4. stage   audience, theater, single
5. volunteer   salary, help, offer
6. piece   quiet, part, cut
7. climb   go up, go out, tree
8. saw   meet, divide, cut

C. First listening.
Look at the pictures and listen to the story. After you listen, tell the class any information you remember about the story.

D. Second listening.
Listen to the story again. Then read these sentences from the story. Which pictures do they tell about? Write the letter of the correct picture in front of each sentence.

_____ 1. Bart is putting his hat on the table.

_____ 2. The rabbits are hopping all over the stage.

_____ 3. Bart is taking off his hat.

_____ 4. Bart is putting his hat back on his head.

_____ 5. Bart is pulling a rabbit out of his hat.

_____ 6. Bart is standing in back of a table. His hat is on.

_____ 7. A young woman is climbing into the box.

_____ 8. Bart is pushing the box back together again.

_____ 9. Bart is sawing the box from top to bottom.

_____ 10. Bart is showing the audience a large, empty box.

_____ 11.   He's pulling the box apart.

_____ 12.   The young woman is climbing out of the box again.

E. Third listening.   Read these sentences. Then, listen to the tape a third time. After you listen, write *T* if the statement is true, *F* if the statement is false.

_____ 1.   Bart is a good magician.

_____ 2.   Bart only knows two tricks.

_____ 3.   The rabbit trick is difficult for Bart.

_____ 4.   The rabbits are under the table.

_____ 5.   Bart is pulling rabbits out of his hat.

_____ 6.   Bart is climbing inside the box.

_____ 7.   The woman who is in the box is a good friend of Bart's.

_____ 8.   At the end of the trick, the woman is in two pieces.

_____ 9.   Bart is teaching the audience how to do tricks.

_____ 10.   Bart enjoys doing tricks for audiences.

F. Comprehension questions.   Listen to each question. Circle the correct answer.

1.   a.   They like the magician to surprise them.
     b.   They want to learn how to do the tricks.
     c.   They like rabbits.

2.   a.   so that the audience can see Bart
     b.   so that Bart can't put anything inside it
     c.   so that Bart can put the rabbits inside it

3.   a.   in his hat
     b.   in his coat
     c.   We don't know. It's a trick.

4.   a.   watch the trick
     b.   climb into the box
     c.   saw him in half

5.   a.   He's sawing the woman in half.
     b.   He's tricking the audience.
     c.   He's doing an easy trick.

6.   a.   the first trick
     b.   the second trick
     c.   all of his tricks

LISTENING DISCRIMINATION

G. Listen and choose.   Listen to each sentence. Circle the preposition you hear.

1. a. back   b. in back   c. in back of
2. a. in   b. on   c. under
3. a. in   b. on   c. under
4. a. in   b. under   c. inside
5. a. up in   b. up on   c. up to
6. a. in   b. on   c. into
7. a. in   b. on   c. into
8. a. in   b. on   c. under
9. a. in . . . to   b. on . . . to   c. from . . . to
10. a. in   b. on   c. into

H. Listen and write.   Listen to each sentence. Write the preposition you hear.

1. _____   6. _____
2. _____   7. _____
3. _____   8. _____
4. _____   9. _____
5. _____   10. _____

I. Listen and decide.   You will hear a statement with a preposition of place. Is the preposition correct or incorrect? Circle *correct* or *incorrect*.

1. correct   incorrect   6. correct   incorrect
2. correct   incorrect   7. correct   incorrect
3. correct   incorrect   8. correct   incorrect
4. correct   incorrect   9. correct   incorrect
5. correct   incorrect   10. correct   incorrect

THE MAGICIAN

J. Cloze.   Fill in each blank with the correct word.

Bart _____ a magician. People love to watch him do tricks, but they never

understand how he does them. These _____ two of his favorites.

First, the rabbit trick. According to Bart, this one _____ simple. In picture A, Bart _____ _____ _____ _____ _____ a table. The table _____ flat; there _____ nothing _____ it or _____ it. In picture B, Bart _____ _____ off his hat and _____ the audience that there _____ nothing _____ it. He _____ _____ the hat _____ the table. Next, Bart _____ _____ a rabbit out of his hat. Not just one rabbit, five of them! The rabbits _____ _____ all over the stage. Finally, in the last picture, Bart _____ _____ his hat back _____ his head again.

Another trick that Bart enjoys _____ the box trick. This one _____ much more difficult. In picture E, Bart _____ _____ the audience a large, empty box. He _____ also _____ for a volunteer to come _____ _____ stage. In picture F, a young woman _____ _____ _____ the box. We can see her head _____ one end, her feet _____ the other. Next, Bart _____ _____ the box _____ half! He _____ _____ the box _____ top _____ bottom. In picture H, he _____ _____ the box apart. The young woman's head _____ _____ the left of the stage, her feet _____ _____ the right. In picture I, Bart _____ _____ the box back together again. And, finally, the young woman _____ _____ _____ _____ the box again, all _____ one piece.

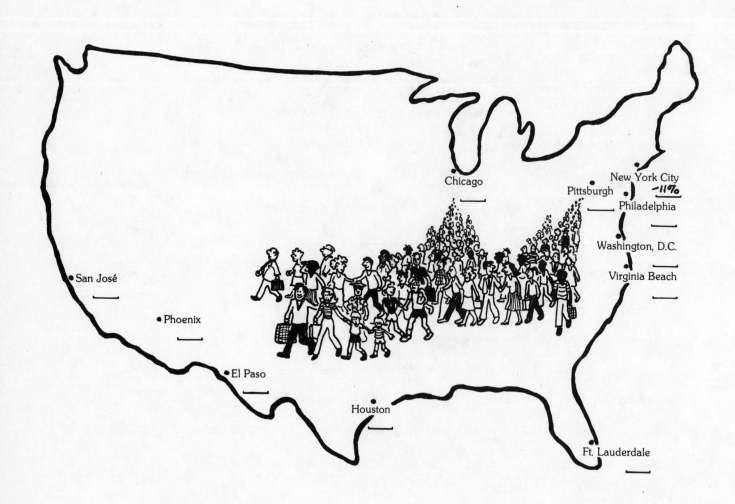

Chicago

Pittsburgh

New York City
-11%

Philadelphia

Washington, D.C.

Virginia Beach

San José

Phoenix

El Paso

Houston

Ft. Lauderdale

CENSUS 3

Focus: **Present continuous tense**

Discussion: **Discuss these questions with your classmates.**

What is a census? Were you ever counted in a census? What are some questions you would see on a census form?

Look at the map of the United States. What area of the country do you live in? Would you like to move to a different area? If so, tell where and why.

Vocabulary: **Repeat each word after the tape.**

census   conduct
residents   is declining
population   is growing
pollution   are choosing

LISTENING COMPREHENSION

A. Fill in. Listen to these sentences. Fill in the new vocabulary words from the list above.

1. The _____ of the United States is about 226 million people.

2. A _____ counts the number of people who live in a country.

3. How many _____ live in this country?

4. How often does the United States _____ a census?

5. The population of the United States _____ larger.

6. Many people _____ to move to a warmer climate.

7.   Cars, factories, and noise cause _____ .

8.   The population of Pennsylvania _____ because many factories have closed.

B. Word association.   Circle the two words that you can associate with each new vocabulary word.

1.   census   count, information, help
2.   residents   school, live, people
3.   population   favorite, people, number
4.   pollution   dirt, smoke, flowers
5.   conduct   direct, letter, supervise
6.   decline   become smaller, go down, feel sick
7.   grow   go up, send, become larger
8.   choose   start, decide, prefer

C. First listening.   Look at the map and listen to the story. After you listen, tell the class any information you remember about the story.

D. Second listening.   Listen to the story again. Show on the map how much the population of each city is up (+) or down (−). Look at New York City as an example. If necessary, the teacher will stop the tape after each sentence with a population number.

E. Third listening.   Read these statements. Then, listen to the tape a third time. After you listen, write *T* if the statement is true; *F* if the statement is false.

_____   1.   The U.S. conducted a census in 1980.

_____   2.   The population of the U.S. is about 23 million people.

_____   3.   More people live in the South than in any other area.

_____   4.   Many people are moving from the South to the North.

_____   5.   The population of New York City is down.

_____   6.   Cities in the South are growing.

_____   7.   The population of Houston is declining.

_____   8.   Many people move to the South because they are looking for jobs.

_____ 9. People are choosing to live in smaller cities.

_____ 10. The population of this area of the country is growing.

F. Comprehension questions. Listen to each question. Circle the correct answer.

1. a. every year
   b. every five years
   c. every ten years
2. a. "Where will you go on vacation next year?"
   b. "How many children do you have?"
   c. "How much money do you have in the bank?"
3. a. Washington, D.C.
   b. El Paso, Texas
   c. New York City
4. a. from the North to the South
   b. from the South to the West
   c. from the West to the South
5. a. They're tired of their jobs.
   b. They want to live in large cities.
   c. They're looking for a warmer climate.
6. a. in 1980
   b. in 1990
   c. in 2000

LISTENING DISCRIMINATION

G. Listen and choose. Listen to each sentence. Circle the verb you hear.

1. a. is declining   b. are declining
2. a. is growing   b. are growing
3. a. is   b. are
4. a. is growing   b. are growing
5. a. is changing   b. are changing
6. a. is moving   b. are moving
7. a. is declining   b. are declining
8. a. is leaving   b. are leaving
9. a. is looking   b. are looking
10. a. is choosing   b. are choosing

H. Listen and write. Listen to each sentence. Write the verb you hear.

1. _____   6. _____
2. _____   7. _____
3. _____   8. _____
4. _____   9. _____
5. _____   10. _____

I. Listen and decide. You will hear a statement in the present continuous tense. Is the grammar correct or incorrect? Circle *correct* or *incorrect*.

1. correct   incorrect   6. correct   incorrect
2. correct   incorrect   7. correct   incorrect
3. correct   incorrect   8. correct   incorrect
4. correct   incorrect   9. correct   incorrect
5. correct   incorrect   10. correct   incorrect

THE CENSUS

J. Cloze. Fill in each blank with the correct word.

Every year the United States conducts a census of the population. A census is a count of the people who live in a city or country. Every family receives a form with questions about family size, income, jobs, etc. They answer questions such as: How many people _____ in your family? Do you live in a house or in an apartment? How long have you been living there? Where did you live before this? Where do you work? How much money do you make? The government uses this information to get a better picture of its residents.

The last census was in 1980. The population of the United States _____ now 226,500,000. The population _____ up 23 million people from 1970. In 1970, the population was 203,000,000.

The census shows that some areas of the United States _____

_____ in population while other areas _____ _____ .

In the past, more people lived in the Northeast and North Central areas. But this

_____ _____ . Now, more people live in the South than in any other

area. People _____ _____ from the North to the South and the West.

The population of northern cities _____ down from 1970. For example, the

population of New York City _____ down 11%, the population of Chicago _____

down 12%. In Pennsylvania, the population of Philadelphia _____ down 14% and the

population of Pittsburgh _____ down 18%. Washington, D.C. has almost 16% less

people. At the same time that northern cities _____ _____ , southern

and western cities _____ _____ . The population of San Jose

_____ up 24%. Phoenix _____ up 33%. In Texas, Houston _____ up 26% and El

Paso _____ up 31%. In Florida, the population of Ft. Lauderdale _____ up 10%.

The population of Virginia Beach _____ up 52%.

 Why _____ people _____ the North? Why _____ they

_____ to the South and West? The number one reason _____ jobs.

Because the South and West _____ _____ , there's a need for

builders, teachers, salespeople, etc. People still want to live in cities, but they

_____ _____ smaller cities. They're tired of crime, traffic, and

pollution. Finally, people say they _____ _____ for a warmer climate.

They _____ _____ away from the cold, toward the sun.

BACK IN TOWN 4

Focus: **Present continuous tense**

Discussion: **Discuss these questions with your classmates.**

In this conversation, two people meet after three years. What are some questions you ask when you meet a friend?

Vocabulary: **Repeat each word after the tape.**

plant   is transferring
so   is managing
how come   is looking forward to
is retiring   dating

LISTENING COMPREHENSION

A. Fill in. Listen to these sentences. Fill in the new vocabulary words from the list above.

1. _____ you're working late tonight?

2. He _____ after working at the company for forty years.

3. I work in New York. My company _____ me to Chicago.

4. The new _____ is going to make computer parts.

5. She doesn't have a boyfriend. She isn't _____ anyone.

6. He _____ his vacation next month.

7. He _____ a store in Texas. He's the boss.

8. I'm living in Florida now. _____ is my sister.

B. Word association.   Circle the two words that you can associate with each new vocabulary word.

1.	plant	company, building, color
2.	so	too, fix, also
3.	how come	who, why, reason
4.	retire	work, sixty-five, car
5.	transfer	change, move, write
6.	manage	company, return, boss
7.	look forward	leave, future, happy
8.	date	go out with, put on, boyfriend

C. First listening.   Look at the picture and listen to the story. After you listen, tell the class any information you remember about the story.

D. Second listening.   George is looking forward to returning to Florida. Read the statements below. Then, listen to the conversation again. As you listen, check the reasons why George is looking forward to returning.

_____ 1.   He's going to work for a new company.

_____ 2.   He's going to manage a new plant.

_____ 3.   His father is retiring.

_____ 4.   He's going to be near his parents.

_____ 5.   He's going to see Sarah.

_____ 6.   He's visiting his parents.

_____ 7.   He's going to see Paul.

E. Third listening.   Read these sentences. Then, listen to the tape a third time. After you listen, write *T* if the statement is true, *F* if the statement is false.

_____ 1.   Sarah is in Texas.

_____ 2.   Sarah is a bookkeeper.

_____ 3.   Sarah is dating Paul.

_____ 4.   Sarah is dating George.

_____ 5.   George's father is retiring.

_____ 6.   George is giving his father a party.

_____ 7. George's company is going to open a new plant in Florida.

_____ 8. George is happy that Sarah isn't dating Paul.

_____ 9. George wants to stay in Texas.

_____ 10. Sarah is going to go to the retirement party with George.

F. Comprehension questions. Listen to each question. Circle the correct answer.

1. a. Texas
   b. Florida
   c. Chicago
2. a. His company is transferring him.
   b. His father is retiring.
   c. His company is opening a new plant.
3. a. George's friend
   b. Sarah's husband
   c. Sarah's old boyfriend
4. a. at the computer company
   b. in town
   c. at the retirement party
5. a. Sarah is divorced.
   b. Sarah is a bookkeeper.
   c. Sarah isn't dating Paul.
6. a. He's going to go out with Sarah.
   b. He's going to forget about Sarah.
   c. He's going to ask Sarah to marry him.

LISTENING DISCRIMINATION

G. Listen and choose. Listen to each sentence. Circle the verb you hear.

1. a. am working   b. is working   c. are working
2. a. am doing   b. is doing   c. are doing
3. a. am dating   b. is dating   c. are dating
4. a. am visiting   b. is visiting   c. are visiting
5. a. am retiring   b. is retiring   c. are retiring
6. a. am giving   b. is giving   c. are giving
7. a. am working   b. is working   c. are working
8. a. am living   b. is living   c. are living
9. a. am transferring   b. is transferring   c. are transferring
10. a. am looking forward b. is looking forward c. are looking forward

H. Listen and write.   Listen to each sentence. Write the verb you hear.

1. _____   6. _____

2. _____   7. _____

3. _____   8. _____

4. _____   9. _____

5. _____   10. _____

I. Listen and decide.   You will hear a statement in the present continuous. Is the grammar correct or incorrect? Circle *correct* or *incorrect*.

1. correct   incorrect   6. correct   incorrect
2. correct   incorrect   7. correct   incorrect
3. correct   incorrect   8. correct   incorrect
4. correct   incorrect   9. correct   incorrect
5. correct   incorrect   10. correct   incorrect

BACK IN TOWN

J. Cloze.   Fill in each blank with the correct word.

George: Sarah! _____ that you?

Sarah: George?

George: Yes! It's been three years!

Sarah: Yes, since you left for Texas.

George: How _____ you? You look great!

Sarah: Thanks. So do you.

George: What _____ you _____ now?

Sarah: I _____ _____ for a small company in town. I _____ a

bookkeeper.

George: And how's Paul?

Sarah: Paul! We _____ not _____ anymore. Not for years.

George: I _____ surprised to hear that.

Sarah: How about you? How come you _____ back in town?

George: I _____ _____ my parents. My father _____

_____ and his company _____ _____ him a

retirement party.

Sarah: That's great. _____ you still _____ for Disk Computers?

George: Yes. Right now I_____ _____ in Texas, but they_____

_____ me back to Florida again soon. They_____ _____

a new plant in Miami and I'm going to manage it.

Sarah: I _____ sure your parents are happy that you _____

_____ .

George: Yes, and I _____ _____ _____ to

coming back again, too. Can I call you next month when I return?

Sarah: Of course! I'd like that. Have a wonderful time at your father's party.

George: Thanks. Goodbye Sarah.

Sarah: Bye, George.

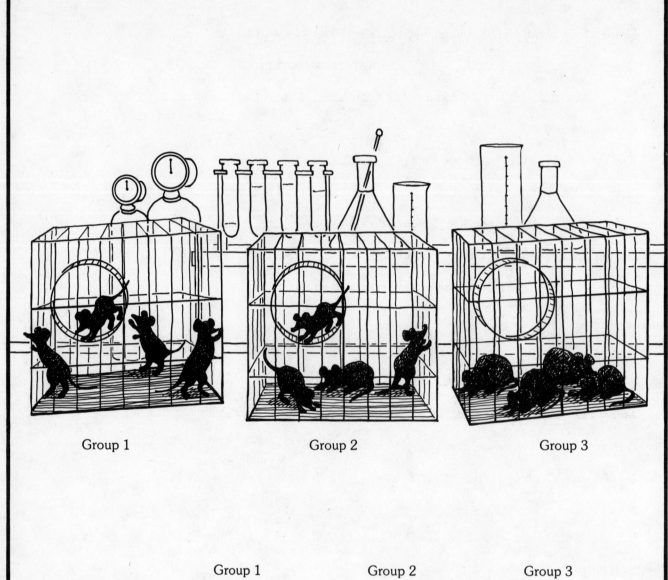

Group 1   Group 2   Group 3

	Group 1	Group 2	Group 3
Amount of Food:	_____	_____	_____
Number of Years:	_____	_____	_____

THE EXPERIMENT   5

Focus: **Present continuous tense**

Discussion: **Discuss these questions with your classmates.**

What is a diet? Do you think you have a good diet? Is there a relationship between what you eat and your health?

Vocabulary: **Repeat each word after the tape.**

laboratory
relationship
diet
health

amount
active
are experimenting
is ongoing

LISTENING COMPREHENSION

A. Fill in.   Listen to these sentences. Fill in the new vocabulary words from the list above.

1.   Scientists _____ with animals.

2.   They have a good _____ with fruit, vegetables, bread, milk, and meat.

3.   His _____ is excellent. He's never sick.

4.   Monkeys are _____ animals. They're always jumping, running, and playing.

5.   A scientist usually works in a _____ .

6.   The experiment _____ . It isn't finished yet.

7.   Ten cups of food is a large _____ to eat.

8.   What is the _____ between smoking and health?

B. Word association.   Circle the two words that you can associate with each new vocabulary word.

1.   laboratory   scientist, experiment, bathroom
2.   relationship   connection, picture, association
3.   diet   end, food, eat
4.   health   body, noise, strong
5.   amount   how much, clothes, quantity
6.   active   movie, busy, moving
7.   experiment   try, test, right
8.   ongoing   at this moment, look at, happening now

C. First listening.   Look at the pictures and listen to the story. After you listen, tell the class any information you remember about the story.

D. Second listening.   Listen to the story again. Then, complete the information under the picture. Write in the amount of food that each group is eating each day. Write in the number of years that each group of mice is living.

E. Third listening.   Read these sentences. Then, listen to the tape a third time. After you listen, write *T* if the statement is true, *F* if the statement is false.

_____   1.   The scientists in this laboratory are experimenting on monkeys.

_____   2.   They are studying the relationship between diet and health.

_____   3.   This is the only experiment in this laboratory.

_____   4.   All three groups are receiving the same amount of food.

_____   5.   The first group is receiving the healthiest food.

_____   6.   The thinner mice are living longer than the normal weight mice.

_____   7.   The mice who are normal weight are living three years.

_____   8.   The heavy mice are sick more often than the thin mice.

_____   9.   The second group of mice is healthy and active.

_____ 10.   The experiments are finished.

F. Comprehension questions. Listen to each question. Circle the correct answer.

1. a. the relationship between mice and diet
   b. the relationship between diet and health
   c. the relationship between amount of food and diet
2. a. the first group *1 cup each day*
   b. the second group *2 cup*
   c. the third group *3 cup*
3. a. They do not have a healthy diet.
   b. They eat only one cup of food a day.
   c. They use the equipment in their cages.
4. a. a year and a half
   b. two years
   c. three years
5. a. the first group
   b. the second group
   c. the third group
6. a. People who eat less will live longer.
   b. People who eat only a cup of food a day will be healthy.
   c. People who eat a healthy diet will not get sick.

LISTENING DISCRIMINATION

G. Listen and choose. Listen to each sentence. Circle the verb you hear.

1. a. learn   b. is learning   c. are learning
2. a. experiment   b. is experimenting   c. are experimenting
3. a. study   b. is studying   c. are studying
4. a. ongoing   b. is ongoing   c. are ongoing
5. a. receive   b. is receiving   c. are receiving
6. a. eat   b. is eating   c. are eating
7. a. play   b. is playing   c. are playing
8. a. use   b. is using   c. are using
9. a. live   b. is living   c. are living
10. a. sleep   b. is sleeping   c. are sleeping

H. Listen and write. Listen to each sentence. Write the verb you hear.

1. _____   6. _____
2. _____   7. _____
3. _____   8. _____
4. _____   9. _____
5. _____   10. _____

I. Listen and decide. You will hear a statement in the present continuous tense. Is the grammar correct or incorrect? Circle *correct* or *incorrect*.

1. correct   incorrect   6. correct   incorrect
2. correct   incorrect   7. correct   incorrect
3. correct   incorrect   8. correct   incorrect
4. correct   incorrect   9. correct   incorrect
5. correct   incorrect   10. correct   incorrect

THE EXPERIMENT

J. Cloze. Fill in each blank with the correct word.

One way that scientists learn about man is by studying animals, such as mice, rats, and monkeys. The scientists in this laboratory _____ _____ on mice. They _____ _____ the relationship between diet and health. At this time, over one hundred experiments _____ _____ in this laboratory.

In this experiment, the scientists _____ _____ the relationship between the amount of food the mice eat and their health. The mice _____ in three groups. All three groups _____ _____ the same healthy diet. But the amount of food that each group is receiving _____ different. The first group _____ _____ one cup of food each day, the second group _____ _____ two cups, and the third group of mice _____ _____ three cups.

After three years, the healthiest group _____ the one that is only eating one cup of food each day. The mice in this group _____ thinner than normal mice. But they _____ more active. Most of the day, they _____ _____ , _____ with one another, and _____ the equipment in their cages. Also, they _____ _____ longer. Mice usually live for two years. Most of the mice in this group _____ still alive after three years.

The second group of mice _____ normal weight. They _____ healthy, too. They _____ active, but not as active as the thinner mice. But they _____ only _____ about two years, not the three years or more of the thinner mice.

The last group of mice _____ _____ more food than the other two groups. Most of the day, these mice _____ _____ or _____ . They _____ not very active. These mice _____ _____ longer than the scientists thought—about a year and a half. But they _____ not as healthy. They _____ sick more often than the other two groups.

The experiment _____ still _____ . The scientists hope to finish their studies in two years.

ROBOTS

Focus: **Future tense (will-won't)**

Discussion: **Discuss these questions with your classmates.**

What are robots? Did you ever see one in operation? If so, what was it doing? What kind of work can robots do well? Which are better workers, robots or people? Explain why.

Vocabulary: **Repeat each word after the tape.**

ingredients	*breaks down*
measure	*roll*
pour	*will go on strike*
mix	*support*

LISTENING COMPREHENSION

A. Fill in. Listen to these sentences. Fill in the new vocabulary words from the list above.

1. The workers _____ for higher pay.

2. Robots can't walk, they _____ around on wheels.

3. If a robot _____ , we will call a mechanic.

4. It is difficult to _____ a family on $200 a week.

5. What's in this cough syrup? Read the _____ on the label.

6. _____ the ingredients together for five minutes.

7. _____ the exact amount, not too much, not too little.

8. Can a robot _____ the syrup into the bottles carefully?

B. Word association.   Circle the two words that you can associate with each new vocabulary word.

1. ingredients   contents, instructions, label
2. measure   cup, try, amount
3. pour   liquid, money, flow
4. mix   clean, stir, cook
5. break down   not work, watch, mechanic
6. roll   move, wheels, eat
7. go on strike   union, stop work, hit
8. support   think, money, help

C. First listening.   Look at the picture and listen to the conversation. After you listen, tell the class any information you remember about the story.

D. Second listening.   Read these sentences. Then, listen to the story again. Write the correct number on each person or robot in the picture. (Note: all pronouns are "he.")

1. He'll pack the bottles into the boxes.
2. He'll mix the ingredients.
3. He'll pour the syrup.
4. He'll program the robots.
5. He'll measure the ingredients.
6. He'll put on the labels.

E. Third listening.   Read these sentences. Then, listen to the tape a third time. After you listen, write *T* if the statement is true, *F* if the statement is false.

_____ 1.   This factory has ten kinds of robots.

_____ 2.   This company makes ten kinds of cough syrup.

_____ 3.   One robot will take the place of four workers.

_____ 4.   In the future, this factory will only need one or two people.

_____ 5.   The boss will program the robots.

_____ 6.   Robots will work on Sundays.

_____ 7.   Robots break down frequently.

_____ 8.   The workers in this factory take vacations.

_____ 9.   The boss will buy robots immediately.

_____ 10. The boss wants robots because most of his workers are lazy.

F. Comprehension questions. Listen to each question. Circle the correct answer.

1. a. the boss
    b. the assistant
    c. the workers

2. a. The boss will tell them.
    b. A mechanic will program them.
    c. A worker will program them.

3. a. A mechanic will fix it.
    b. A worker will fix it.
    c. The boss will fix it.

4. a. They don't know how to make cough syrup.
    b. They sometimes break down.
    c. They come to work late.

5. a. They can work longer than people.
    b. They are very expensive.
    c. They are very intelligent.

6. a. They will help the robots.
    b. They will lose their jobs.
    c. They will go on strike.

LISTENING DISCRIMINATION

G. Listen and choose. Listen to each sentence. Circle the verb you hear. Several of the verbs are negatives.

	a.	b.	c.
1.	make	will make	won't make
2.	measure	will measure	won't measure
3.	pour	will pour	won't pour
4.	program	will program	won't program
5.	type	will type	won't type
6.	call in	will call in	won't call in
7.	have	will have	won't have
8.	go on strike	will go on strike	won't go on strike
9.	need	will need	won't need
10.	need	will need	won't need

H. Listen and write. Listen to each sentence. Write the verb you hear. All of the verbs are in the future tense; several are negative.

1. _____   6. _____

2. _____   7. _____

3. _____   8. _____

4. _____   9. _____

5. _____   10. _____

I. Listen and decide. You will hear a statement in the future tense. Is the grammar correct or incorrect? Circle *correct* or *incorrect*.

1. correct   incorrect   6. correct   incorrect
2. correct   incorrect   7. correct   incorrect
3. correct   incorrect   8. correct   incorrect
4. correct   incorrect   9. correct   incorrect
5. correct   incorrect   10. correct   incorrect

ROBOTS

J. Cloze. Fill in each blank with the correct word.

Boss: Robots? Why _____ you _____ about robots? We _____ a small company, we make cough syrup. We only have twenty workers. Robots are fine for large factories, not small ones like ours.

Assistant: Boss, small companies can use robots, too. They _____ great workers.

Boss: I don't know. Talk to me about them ten years from now.

Assistant: Listen, this _____ a simple operation here. We make ten different kinds of cough syrup. But each operation only has five steps, so we _____ only _____ five robots. One robot _____ _____ the ingredients, and a second robot _____ _____ them. A third robot _____ _____ the syrup into the bottles. Then a fourth robot _____ _____ on the labels. The last robot _____ _____ the bottles into boxes. Right now, we have twenty workers doing those jobs.

Boss: But each kind of syrup _____ different. How _____ these robots _____ what do do?

Assistant: We _____ tell them. One worker _____ _____ the robots. She _____ just _____ the orders into a computer. She _____ _____ the robots what ingredients to use, how long to mix them, and which labels to use.

Boss: And what happens when one of the robots breaks down?

Assistant: They don't break down very often. And the robotics company _____ _____ a mechanic here within an hour.

Boss: I just can't picture it. What _____ we _____ here? A quiet building with robots rolling around doing the work?

Assistant: That _____ it! And these robots _____ great workers. They _____ never _____ to work late and they _____ _____ _____ sick. They _____ _____ vacations. They _____ _____ twenty-four hours a day, seven days a week, 365 days a year. And they _____ _____ _____ _____ .

Boss: I don't know. It sounds like a good idea, but I need time to think. What about the men and women who work here now? Most of them _____ good workers. They have families to support.

Assistant: Boss, that _____ the only problem. We _____ _____ them anymore.

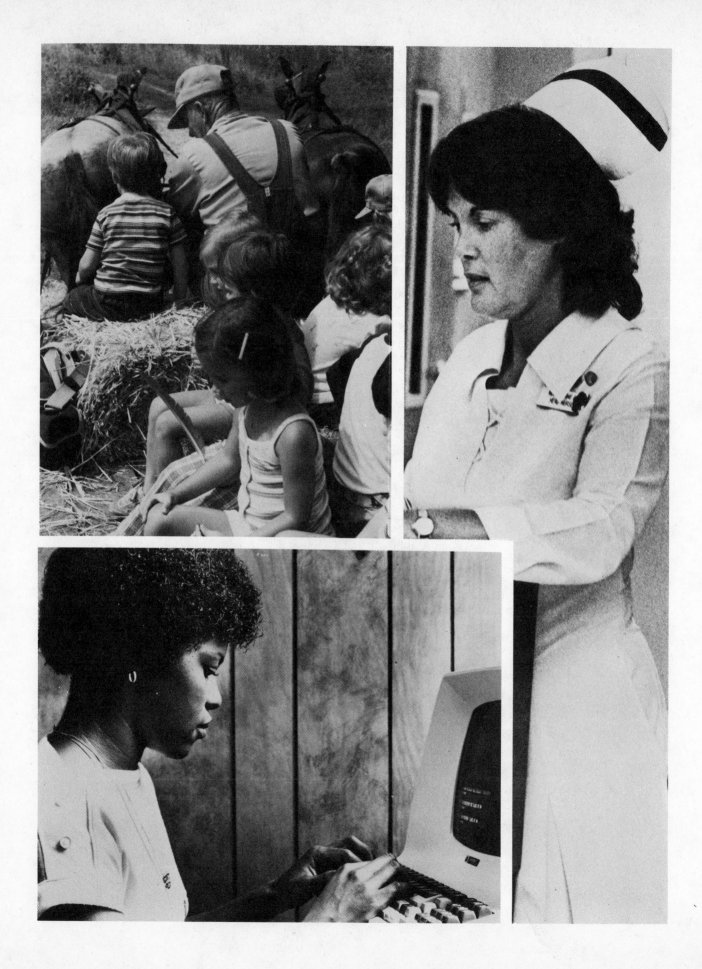

JOB OUTLOOK 7

Focus: **Future tense (will)**

Discussion: **Discuss these questions with your classmates.**

What kind of work do you do (or what kind of work are you preparing for)? What is the future for your kind of work? Will workers be in demand in your kind of work ten years from now? What kinds of jobs have an excellent or poor future? Why?

Vocabulary: **Repeat each word after the tape.**

repairs
in demand
machines
spend

describes
will lose
will go out of business
publishes

LISTENING COMPREHENSION

A. Fill in. Listen to these sentences. Fill in the new vocabulary words from the list above.

1. Cashiers will be _____ in stores and supermarkets.

2. Because families are having fewer children, some teachers _____ their jobs.

3. Small farms do not make much money and many _____ .

4. The government _____ a book which tells about the future of many jobs.

5. This book _____ job duties, working conditions, and salary.

6. Families with working mothers will have more money to _____ .

7. In the future, _____ will do some jobs that people do now.

8. Older cars need more _____ than newer cars.

B. Word association. Circle the two words that you can associate with each new vocabulary word.

1. repairs   fix, parts, word
2. in demand   needed, type, necessary
3. machine   color, equipment, engine
4. spend   try, money, use
5. describe   walk, tell, report
6. lose (a job)   not work, work hard, unemployment
7. go out of business   open, close, end
8. publish   try, book, print

C. First listening. Look at the pictures and listen to the story. After you listen, tell the class any information you remember about the story.

D. Second listening. Read the list of occupations below. Is the job outlook excellent, good, or poor? Listen to the tape again and check the job outlook for the future.

	Excellent	Good	Poor
1. Auto mechanic		✓	
2. Computer programmer			
3. Cashier			
4. Cook or chef			
5. Farmer			
6. High school teacher			
7. Mailman and mailwoman			
8. Nurse			
9. Painter			
10. Radio and tv technician			

E. Third listening. Read these sentences. Then, listen to the tape a third time. After you listen, write *T* if the statement is true, *F* if the statement is false.

_____ 1. The *Occupational Outlook Handbook* tells about the future of over 250 jobs.

_____ 2. It tells how many openings there will be for a job.

_____ 3. No one knows the future of any job.

_____ 4. The job outlook for cashiers is poor.

_____ 5. Families with working mothers will eat out more often.

_____ 6. Most cooks will find jobs.

_____ 7. Schools will need more teachers.

_____ 8. There will be a need for more nurses because people are living longer.

_____ 9. Some mailmen and mailwomen will lose their jobs.

_____ 10. In the future, families will buy more electronic equipment.

F. Comprehension questions. Listen to each question. Circle the correct answer.

1. a. the companies that are looking for workers
   b. job duties and salary
   c. only those jobs which need a college education
2. a. If a person becomes a cook, she will definitely find a job.
   b. If a person becomes a cook, she will probably find a job.
   c. If a person becomes a cook, she probably won't find a job.
3. a. People will keep their cars longer.
   b. People will buy more new cars.
   c. Every family in this country has a car.
4. a. The population is declining.
   b. Farmers are using more machines.
   c. Farms are becoming smaller.
5. a. in the East
   b. in the South
   c. in the North
6. a. high school teacher
   b. auto mechanic
   c. radio and tv technician

LISTENING DISCRIMINATION

G. Listen and choose.   Listen to each sentence. Circle the verb you hear.

1. a. describes   b. is describing   c. will describe
2. a. talks   b. is talking   c. will talk
3. a. keep   b. are keeping   c. will keep
4. a. grows   b. is growing   c. will grow
5. a. work   b. are working   c. will work
6. a. need   b. are needing   c. will need
7. a. face   b. are facing   c. will face
8. a. live   b. are living   c. will live
9. a. open   b. are opening   c. will open
10. a. buy   b. are buying   c. will buy

H. Listen and write.   Listen to each sentence. Write the future verb you hear.

1. _____   6. _____
2. _____   7. _____
3. _____   8. _____
4. _____   9. _____
5. _____   10. _____

I. Listen and decide.   You will hear a statement in the future tense. Is the grammar correct or incorrect? Circle *correct* or *incorrect.*

1. correct   incorrect   6. correct   incorrect
2. correct   incorrect   7. correct   incorrect
3. correct   incorrect   8. correct   incorrect
4. correct   incorrect   9. correct   incorrect
5. correct   incorrect   10. correct   incorrect

JOB OUTLOOK

J. Cloze.   Fill in each blank with the correct word.

The job outlook for mechanics is good. The number of cars _____

_____ to grow. Because cars are so expensive, people _____

_____ their cars longer. Their cars _____ _____

more repairs.

Computer programmers _____ also _____ in demand and the

job outlook is excellent. Big and small companies _____ _____

computers for much of their work.

The outlook for cashiers in stores, supermarkets, theaters, etc. is excellent. There

_____ _____ a need for more than half a million new cashiers in the

next ten years.

The demand for cooks and chefs _____ also _____ , the outlook

is good in this area. The population _____ _____ and so more

people _____ _____ out. Also, more mothers

_____ _____ and families _____ _____ more

money to spend.

The outlook for farmers is poor. Farms _____ _____ larger and

use better machinery to plant food. Many small farms _____ _____ _____

_____ _____ .

The future for high school teachers is poor, also. Because families _____

_____ fewer children, schools _____ _____ fewer

teachers. There _____ _____ a need for math and science teachers, but some

history and English teachers _____ _____ their jobs.

The mailmen and mailwomen who deliver the mail every day face a poor job future,

too. Post offices _____ _____ more machines.

The job outlook for nurses is excellent for both registered nurses and licensed

practical nurses. The population _____ _____ and people _____

_____ longer.

Friends don't let friends drive drunk.

If your friend has had too much to drink, he doesn't have to drive.
Here are three ways to keep your friend alive . . .

drive your friend home

have your friend sleep over

call a cab

U.S. Department of Transportation

**National Highway Traffic Safety
Administration**

DRUNK DRIVER   8

Focus: **Future tense (going to)**

Discussion: **Discuss these questions with your classmates.**

You are at a party and a friend drinks too much. He's going to drive home. What do you do?

What is the penalty in your state for drunk driving?

Vocabulary: **Repeat each word after the tape.**

duty	prevent
injuries	is weaving
toll booth	issue a summons
breath	is going to suspend

LISTENING COMPREHENSION

A. Fill in.   Listen to these sentences. Fill in the new vocabulary words from the list above.

1. All drivers on that highway pay a quarter at the _____ .

2. Try to _____ accidents before they happen.

3. The _____ test shows that Joe has a lot of liquor in his body.

4. The policeman is going to _____ that driver

   _____ for speeding.

5. The officers are on special _____ . They're looking for drunk drivers.

6. That man isn't driving in a straight line. He _____ in and out.

7. The judge _____ his license. He can't drive for two months.

8. My friend received serious _____ in the accident. She's still in the hospital.

B. Word association.   Circle the two words that you can associate with each new vocabulary word.

1. duty   job, late, assignment
2. injury   hurt, accident, country
3. toll booth   telephone, money, highway
4. breath   mouth, die, air
5. prevent   stop, come after, come before
6. weave   in and out, not straight, over
7. issue a summons   ticket, court, question
8. suspend   speak, stop, take away

C. First listening.   Look at the picture and listen to the story. After you listen, tell the class any information you remember about the story.

D. Second listening.   Read these questions. Then, listen to the story again. As you listen, write the correct number in the blank.

_____ 1. How many officers are on special duty?

_____ 2. How many people are going to die this weekend from accidents caused by drunk drivers?

_____ 3. How many people are going to receive serious injuries?

_____ 4. How much is Joe's fine going to be?

_____ 5. For how long is the judge going to suspend Joe's license?

E. Third listening.   Read these sentences. Then, listen to the tape a third time. After you listen, write T if the statement is true, F if the statement is false.

_____ 1. It's a holiday weekend.

_____ 2. Joe is drinking at a party.

_____ 3. He's going to wait for a few hours before he drives home.

_____ 4. His sister is going to drive him home from the party.

_____ 5. It is safe to drink, then drive slowly.

_____ 6. Officer Williams is watching for drunk drivers.

_____ 7. Joe speeds into the toll booth area.

_____ 8. Joe walks along the white line easily.

_____ 9. Joe is going to appear in court.

_____ 10. Joe can't drive for sixty days.

F. Comprehension questions. Listen to each question. Circle the correct answer.

1. a. during the day when the traffic is the heaviest
    b. in the early evening when many people go out for dinner
    c. late at night when people are driving home from parties
2. a. 40
    b. 400
    c. 4,000
3. a. Joe is tired.
    b. Joe had too many drinks.
    c. Joe feels sick.
4. a. He had an accident.
    b. He's weaving in and out.
    c. He didn't pay the toll.
5. a. walk along a white line
    b. take a breath test
    c. both a and b
6. a. $400 fine
    b. $400 fine and sixty days in jail
    c. $400 fine and 60 days not driving

LISTENING DISCRIMINATION

G. Listen and choose. Listen to each sentence. Circle the verb you hear.

1. a. am going to die   b. is going to die   c. are going to die
2. a. am going to receive   b. is going to receive   c. are going to receive
3. a. am going to leave   b. is going to leave   c. are going to leave
4. a. am going to be   b. is going to be   c. are going to be
5. a. am going to drive   b. is going to drive   c. are going to drive

6. a. am going to drive   b. is going to drive   c. are going to drive
7. a. am going to appear   b. is going to appear   c. are going to appear
8. a. am going to receive   b. is going to receive   c. are going to receive
9. a. am going to suspend   b. is going to suspend   c. are going to suspend
10. a. am going to try   b. is going to try   c. are going to try

H. Listen and write. Listen to each sentence. Write the verb you hear.

1. _____   6. _____
2. _____   7. _____
3. _____   8. _____
4. _____   9. _____
5. _____   10. _____

I. Listen and decide. You will hear a statement in the future tense. Is the grammar correct or incorrect? Circle *correct* or *incorrect*.

1. correct   incorrect   6. correct   incorrect
2. correct   incorrect   7. correct   incorrect
3. correct   incorrect   8. correct   incorrect
4. correct   incorrect   9. correct   incorrect
5. correct   incorrect   10. correct   incorrect

DRUNK DRIVER

J. Cloze. Fill in each blank with the correct word.

It's a holiday weekend. The police officers _____ _____ in a hot room receiving instructions from their captain. One of these officers _____ Ed Williams. He and ten other officers _____ on special duty. This weekend alone, over 400 people _____ _____ _____ _____ from accidents caused by drunk drivers. Over 4,000 people _____ _____ _____ _____ serious injuries, all caused by drunk drivers. The officers _____ _____ _____ _____ to prevent these accidents before they happen.

Meanwhile, Joe Forest _____ _____ himself at a family party. It

_____ _____ late and he_____ _____ his sister

that he _____ _____ _____ _____ . She _____

_____ him to stay and wait a few hours before he drives. "Don't worry. I

_____ _____ _____ _____ fine. I_____ _____ _____ _____

slowly. I only had a few drinks."

Officer Williams _____ at a toll booth, watching cars enter the area. A green Ford

_____ _____ , weaving from left to right. Officer Williams stops the

car and tells Joe to get out. He asks Joe to walk along the white line. He can't do it. Joe also

fails the breath test. Officer Williams _____ _____ Joe that he

_____ _____ _____ _____ him a summons. And he can't

drive his car home. Joe calls his sister. She_____ _____ _____ _____ and

_____ him home.

This was Joe's first offense. He _____ _____ _____ _____

in court next week. He _____ _____ _____ _____ a $400

fine. The judge _____ also_____ _____ _____ his license for

sixty days. This first time, other drivers were lucky. Joe didn't kill them. But what about the

future, _____ Joe _____ _____ _____ drinking and driving?

SHOPLIFTING   9

Focus: **Future tense**

Discussion: **Discuss these questions with your classmates.**

What is shoplifting? Did you ever see anyone stopped for shoplifting? What is the fine and/or penalty for shoplifting?

Vocabulary: **Repeat each word after the tape.**

bathing suit
credit card
dressing room
babysits

try on
keep
hide
catch

LISTENING COMPREHENSION

A. Fill in.   Listen to these sentences. Fill in the new vocabulary words from the list above.

1.   When I don't have enough money with me, I use my_____ .

2.   She'll buy a _____ to wear at the beach.

3.   The store owner will _____ her if she tries to take any clothes.

4.   She'll _____ many dresses before she buys one.

5.   Those pants look big. Try them on in the _____ .

6.   She's going to _____ a bathing suit under her clothes.

7.   On the weekends, she_____ for a family with two children.

8.   She'll _____ the bathing suit she likes best.

49

B. Word association. Circle the two words that you can associate with each new vocabulary word.

1. bathing suit   swim, water, soap
2. credit card   play, money, charge
3. dressing room   store, dinner, try on
4. babysit   children, read, take care of
5. try on   put down, size, clothes
6. keep   take, watch, hold
7. hide   cover, meet, secret
8. catch   try, find, discover

C. First listening. Look at the picture and listen to the story. After you listen, tell the class any information you remember about the story.

D. Second listening. Listen to the story again. Then read the sentences below. Who do you think would say each sentence? Write the letter in front of each sentence.

A = Ann   S = Store clerk
B = Berta   M = Ann's mother

_____ 1. That clerk is watching me.

_____ 2. Stop being so nervous.

_____ 3. I'm going to keep this one. They'll never know.

_____ 4. Girls, would you please step over here a moment.

_____ 5. Why did I ever come along with you?

_____ 6. No, I have nothing on under my clothes.

_____ 7. Please don't call my mother.

_____ 8. Oh, no! I'll drive over to the store immediately.

_____ 9. She'll pay for the bathing suit.

_____ 10. This is the first time and she's very young. We won't call the police this time.

E. Third listening. Read these sentences. Then, listen to the tape a third time. After you listen, write *T* if the statement is true, *F* if the statement is false.

_____ 1. Ann is poor.

_____ 2. Ann has about twenty dollars with her.

_____ 3. Ann is going to steal a bathing suit.

_____ 4. Berta is just going to look at the bathing suits.

_____ 5. Ann is going to use her mother's credit card.

_____ 6. Ann is going to take four bathing suits into the dressing room.

_____ 7. Ann is going to keep five bathing suits.

_____ 8. Berta thinks that someone will see them.

_____ 9. Ann is going to tell her mother that she bought the bathing suit.

_____ 10. Berta will come into the store with Ann.

F. Comprehension questions. Listen to each question. Circle the correct answer.

1. a. She's going to use her mother's credit card.
    b. She's going to steal it.
    c. She's going to use her money from babysitting.

2. a. none
    b. one
    c. two

3. a. She thinks it's a good idea.
    b. She doesn't think it's a good idea.
    c. She's going to think about it.

4. a. She's going to stay with her.
    b. She's going to shoplift with her.
    c. She's going to go home.

5. a. She's going to put it in a bag.
    b. She's going to hide it in some other clothes.
    c. She's going to wear it out of the store under her clothes.

6. a. Berta gave it to her.
    b. She stole it.
    c. She got the money from babysitting.

LISTENING DISCRIMINATION

G. Listen and choose. Listen to each sentence. Circle the verb you hear.

1. a. will look   b. is going to look
2. a. will walk   b. is going to walk
3. a. will look   b. is going to look
4. a. will keep   b. is going to keep
5. a. will hide   b. am going to hide
6. a. will have   b. am going to have
7. a. will catch   b. are going to catch
8. a. will try   b. are going to try
9. a. will come   b. am going to come
10. a. will say   b. is going to say

H. Listen and write. Listen to each sentence. Write the verb you hear.

1. _____   .6 _____
2. _____   7. _____
3. _____   8. _____
4. _____   9. _____
5. _____   10. _____

I. Listen and decide. You will hear a statement in the future tense. Is the grammar correct or incorrect? Circle *correct* or *incorrect*.

1. correct   incorrect   6. correct   incorrect
2. correct   incorrect   7. correct   incorrect
3. correct   incorrect   8. correct   incorrect
4. correct   incorrect   9. correct   incorrect
5. correct   incorrect   10. correct   incorrect

SHOPLIFTING

J. Cloze. Fill in each blank with the correct word.

Two teenage girls _____ _____ together.

A: Let's go shopping for bathing suits, Berta.

B: Okay. But I _____ just _____ _____ _____ . I don't have any money with me.

A: I don't, either. But I _____ _____ _____ _____ out of that store with a new bathing suit.

B: How? _____ you _____ _____ _____ your mother's credit card?

A: No. Listen, I have an idea. We _____ _____ into the store and _____ at the suits and _____ lots of them. Then, we _____ each _____ the one we like the best. We _____ just _____ them out of the store under our clothes. No one _____ _____ us and we _____ _____ to pay a penny.

B: But they give you a number when you walk into the dressing room.

A: I know. I _____ _____ _____ _____ one bathing suit inside another one. I _____ _____ the number four, but I _____ really _____ five suits.

B: Are you serious, Ann? They _____ _____ _____ _____ you.

A: No, they _____ . _____ you _____ _____ _____ it, too?

B: I don't think so. But I _____ _____ with you. What _____ your mother _____ _____ _____ when she sees your new bathing suit?

A: I _____ _____ her that I got the money from babysitting.

B: You know, Ann, I don't really think that this is such a good idea.

A: So? Are you _____ or not?

B: I _____ _____ .

KANGAROOS

Focus: **Present tense**

Discussion: **Discuss these questions with your classmates.**

Did you ever see a kangaroo? Where? Describe it. What information can you tell the class about kangaroos?

Vocabulary: **Repeat each word after the tape.**

herd	*nipple*
hind	*develops*
marsupial	*nurses*
pouch	*searching*

LISTENING COMPREHENSION

A. Fill in.   Listen to these sentences. Fill in the new vocabulary words from the list above.

1.   Kangaroos have small front legs and large _____ legs.

2.   About twenty-five kangaroos live together in that _____ .

3.   Kangaroos move from place to place, _____ for food.

4.   A _____ is an animal which has a pouch.

5.   A baby kangaroo lives in its mother's _____ .

6.   A baby kangaroo grows and _____ in its mother's pouch.

7.   In the pouch, the baby takes hold of its mother's _____ .

8.   With the nipple in its mouth, the baby _____ for many weeks.

B. Word association.   Circle the two words that you can associate with each new vocabulary word.

1. herd   group, together, ear
2. hind   nice, back, rear
3. marsupial   pouch, kangaroo, flower
4. pouch   hit, pocket, carry
5. nipple   mother, milk, time
6. develop   grow, form, sleep
7. nurse   baby, milk, rich
8. search   look, hurt, find

C. First listening.   Look at the picture and listen to the story. After you listen, tell the class any information you remember about the story.

D. Second listening.   Read the statements below. Then, listen to the story again. As you listen, complete the information in each statement.

1. Kangaroos are about _____ feet tall.

2. They weigh about _____ pounds.

3. About _____ animals live in a herd.

4. Kangaroos can jump _____ feet.

5. They can move _____ miles an hour.

E. Third listening.   Read these sentences. Then, listen to the tape a third time. After you listen, write *T* if the statement is true, *F* if the statement is false.

_____ 1. A kangaroo is about the size of a man.

_____ 2. Kangaroos use their hind legs for jumping.

_____ 3. Kangaroos live together in small families.

_____ 4. A herd moves from place to place.

_____ 5. A kangaroo carries food in its pouch.

_____ 6. At birth, a baby kangaroo can see.

_____ 7. The baby lives in the pouch for one year.

_____ 8. The baby nurses in the pouch.

_____ 9. A young kangaroo is called a joey.

_____ 10. In the United States, kangaroos move about in freedom.

F. Comprehension questions. Listen to each question. Circle the correct answer.

1. a. It jumps away.
   b. It fights.
   c. It stands very quietly.
2. a. because kangaroos live in herds
   b. because kangaroos are always looking for food
   c. because kangaroos are so large
3. a. holding food
   b. jumping
   c. eating food
4. a. It's fully formed.
   b. It's not developed.
   c. Its front and hind legs are well developed.
5. a. It climbs into its mother's pouch.
   b. It's born in the pouch.
   c. The mother kangaroo puts the baby in the pouch.
6. a. after a few weeks
   b. after thirty to forty days
   c. after six months

LISTENING DISCRIMINATION

G. Listen and choose. Listen to each sentence. Circle the verb you hear.

1. a. move   b. moves
2. a. weigh   b. weighs
3. a. stand   b. stands
4. a. have   b. has
5. a. move   b. moves
6. a. have   b. has
7. a. live   b. lives
8. a. climb   b. climbs
9. a. grow   b. grows
10. a. live   b. lives

H. Listen and write.   Listen to each sentence. Write the verb you hear.

1. _____   6. _____

2. _____   7. _____

3. _____   8. _____

4. _____   9. _____

5. _____   10. _____

I. Listen and decide.   You will hear a statement in the present tense. Is the grammar correct or incorrect? Circle *correct* or *incorrect*.

1. correct   incorrect   6. correct   incorrect
2. correct   incorrect   7. correct   incorrect
3. correct   incorrect   8. correct   incorrect
4. correct   incorrect   9. correct   incorrect
5. correct   incorrect   10. correct   incorrect

KANGAROOS

J. Cloze.   Fill in each blank with the correct word.

Australia _____ the home of the kangaroo. In most parts of the world, a person

must go to a zoo to see a kangaroo. In Australia, kangaroos _____ about

in freedom in the forests and on the plains. Long ago, kangaroos were giants. They were

almost ten feet tall. Today, kangaroos _____ about the size of a man. They _____

five to six feet tall and _____ about 150 pounds. Kangaroos

_____ on their large hind legs. They _____ these hind

legs for jumping and, if necessary, for fighting. Close to the kangaroo's body _____

small front legs. These are for finding and holding food.

Kangaroos _____ in herds of twelve or more animals. Some herds

_____ more than fifty kangaroos. A herd _____ no

fixed home, it _____ from place to place, searching for food. If

something_____ the herd, the kangaroos_____ away,

all at once. Kangaroos can jump twenty-five feet or more and they can move twenty-five miles per hour.

    A kangaroo _____ a marsupial, which means it _____ a pouch. A baby kangaroo _____ inside its mother for only thirty to forty days. At birth, the baby _____ only about one inch long and it _____ _____ fully formed. Its eyes and ears are closed, it _____ no fur, and its hind legs are not developed. This small baby _____ up its mother's body and into her pouch. It _____ hold of a nipple and _____ there for many weeks, nursing and developing. Soon, its eyes _____ and its ears _____ . It _____ fur. Finally, the baby kangaroo _____ go of the nipple and _____ outside. At six months of age, the young kangaroo _____ the pouch. Now, it _____ called a joey.

TOY WORLD 11

Focus: **Present tense**

Discussion: **Discuss these questions with your classmates.**

Do you (or does one of your friends) work in a factory? What does the factory manufacture? What do you do? How many shifts operate at the factory? What is the busiest time of the year?

Vocabulary: **Repeat each word after the tape.**

temperature
assembly line
shift
load

manufactures
get laid off
fit
assemble

LISTENING COMPREHENSION

A. Fill in. Listen to these sentences. Fill in the new vocabulary words from the list above.

1. I work the second _____ at the factory, from 3:00 to 11:00.

2. Ford Motor Company _____ cars.

3. It's cold today. The _____ is 20°.

4. When work is slow at our company, many workers_____ .

5. This factory receives radio parts from different companies. The workers here

   _____ the radios.

6. This part is too big. It doesn't _____ into the hole.

7. Two men take the boxes and _____ them onto a truck.

8. Each worker on an _____ does a different job.

B. Word association.   Circle the two words that you can associate with each new vocabulary word.

1.	manufacture	make, build, help
2.	fit	size, pretty, go together
3.	assemble	fight, put together, parts
4.	get laid off	unemployment, lose a job, study
5.	temperature	hot, angry, cold
6.	assembly line	many workers, parts, pencil
7.	shift	hours, read, time
8.	load	heavy, relax, carry

C. First listening.   Look at the picture and listen to the story. After you listen, tell the class any information you remember about the story.

D. Second listening.   Listen to the story again. Write the name of each worker on the picture. Then, match the workers and their jobs.

1.	Bill and James	a.	installs a voice box.
2.	Olga	b.	assemble the dolls.
3.	Tony and Marta	c.	put the parts on the line.
4.	Ana	d.	loads the truck.
5.	George	e.	dresses the dolls.
6.	Mark	f.	packs the dolls in boxes.

E. Third listening.   Read these statements. Then, listen to the tape a third time. After you listen, write *T* if the statement is true, *F* if the statement is false.

_____   1.   It's winter at Toy World.

_____   2.   There are many assembly lines in this factory.

_____   3.   The parts arrive in different boxes.

_____   4.   Bill and James put all the heads in one box, all the bodies in another.

_____   5.   The dolls can say "Bye-bye."

_____   6.   If a part doesn't fit, there are extra parts next to the line.

_____   7.   Ana puts pretty dresses on the dolls.

_____   8.   Children can see into the box because the front is plastic.

_____   9.   Toy World is very busy in December.

_____   10.   The toys have to be on toy shelves by September.

F. Comprehension questions. Listen to each question. Circle the correct answer.

1. a. only dolls
   b. parts for dolls
   c. toys

2. a. dresses
   b. pajamas
   c. hats

3. a. "Mommy"
   b. "Bye-bye"
   c. "Night-night"

4. a. by November
   b. by July
   c. by May

5. a. They are called back to work.
   b. They get laid off.
   c. They work hard, getting ready for Christmas.

6. a. one
   b. two
   c. three

LISTENING DISCRIMINATION

G. Listen and choose. Listen to each sentence. Circle the verb you hear.

1. a. manufactures   b. manufacture
2. a. assembles   b. assemble
3. a. arrives   b. arrive
4. a. unpacks   b. unpack
5. a. installs   b. install
6. a. assembles   b. assemble
7. a. has   b. have
8. a. puts   b. put
9. a. operates   b. operate
10. a. gets laid off   b. get laid off

H. Listen and write.   Listen to each sentence. Write the verb you hear.

1. _____   6. _____

2. _____   7. _____

3. _____   8. _____

4. _____   9. _____

5. _____   10. _____

I. Listen and decide.   You will hear a statement in the present tense. Is the grammar correct or incorrect? Circle *correct* or *incorrect*.

1. correct   incorrect   6. correct   incorrect
2. correct   incorrect   7. correct   incorrect
3. correct   incorrect   8. correct   incorrect
4. correct   incorrect   9. correct   incorrect
5. correct   incorrect   10. correct   incorrect

TOY WORLD

J. Cloze.   Fill in each blank with the correct word.

It's July. The temperature is 89°. The workers at Toy World _____

busy, getting ready for Christmas. Toy World _____ children's toys. It

_____ many short assembly lines. This area _____

dolls. The doll parts _____ from Hong Kong. They_____

in large boxes, one for arms, another for legs, one for bodies, another for heads. Bill and

James_____ the boxes and_____ the parts on the line.

They put a head, a body, one left arm, one right arm, one left leg, and one right leg in each

box. Olga _____ a voice box in the back of each doll. The dolls can say

"Mommy," "Daddy," and "night-night." Then, Tony and Marta _____

the dolls. Sometimes a part _____ _____ , so there _____ extra

parts next to the line. Then Ana _____ the dolls. She

_____ pink pajamas on some dolls, yellow pajamas on others.

George _____ the dolls in boxes. The front of each box is clear plastic so that children and their parents can see the doll in the box. He _____ the smaller boxes into a larger one. Mark _____ these boxes onto a truck.

Toy World is busy from May to November. During these months, it _____ three shifts. But all the toys _____ to be on store shelves by November. From December to April, business is slow and many workers _____ laid off. Usually, only one shift _____ .

ADULT DAY CARE   12

Focus: **Contrast present tense and present continuous tense**

Discussion: **Discuss these questions with your classmates.**

Do you have a grandmother, grandfather, or other relative who is over eighty years old? Where does he/she live? Does anyone take care of him/her? Is he/she forgetful? What do you think adult day care is? Why is it necessary?

Vocabulary: **Repeat each word after the tape.**

patient	therapy
artificial	stroke
forgetful	is recovering
elderly	are participating

LISTENING COMPREHENSION

A. Fill in.   Listen to these sentences. Fill in the new vocabulary words from the list above.

1. John needed physical _____ to help him walk again after his accident.

2. My father _____ quickly after his accident. He'll be home from the hospital next week.

3. Many families _____ in this program.

4. After he lost his arm in the accident, he received an _____ one.

5. My mother is becoming _____. She can't remember people's names.

6. The woman who lives above us is _____. She's over ninety years old.

7. After his _____ , John couldn't move the left side of his body.

8. After his operation, he was a _____ in the hospital for two weeks.

B. Word association.   Circle the two words that you can associate with each new vocabulary word.

1. patient   hospital, kind, sick
2. artificial   beautiful, not real, man-made
3. forgetful   can't remember, tired, fail
4. elderly   old, grandparent, prepare
5. therapy   help, hat, recover
6. stroke   disagree, heart, paralyzed
7. recover   put on, get better, improve
8. participate   take part in, belong to, answer

C. First listening.   Look at the picture and listen to the story. After you listen, tell the class any information you remember about the story.

D. Second listening.   Listen to the story again. Then, read these activities. Which activities do you think an Adult Day Care Center would offer?

_____ 1. swimming   _____ 6. watching movies

_____ 2. cooking   _____ 7. playing games

_____ 3. taking short walks   _____ 8. playing baseball

_____ 4. painting   _____ 9. sewing

_____ 5. driving lessons   _____ 10. looking for a job

E. Third listening.   Read these sentences. Then, listen to the tape a third time. After you listen, write *T* if the sentence is true, *F* if the sentence is false.

_____   1. David Brown lives in a nursing home.

_____   2. Mrs. Brown doesn't want to leave her husband alone.

_____   3. Ann Ramos helps her daughter with the housework.

_____   4. Adult Day Care patients can sleep in the hospital.

_____ 5. Some patients only come a few mornings a week.

_____ 6. Some patients are recovering from accidents.

_____ 7. The patients enjoy one another's company.

_____ 8. All the patients receive physical therapy.

_____ 9. There are many different activities for the patients.

_____ 10. Most of the patients are elderly.

F. Comprehension questions. Listen to each question. Circle the correct answer.

1. a. He started a fire in their apartment.
    b. She doesn't want to stay with him all day.
    c. She's worried that he might hurt himself.

2. a. Ann sits next to her daughter when she reads.
    b. Ann follows her out of the house when she takes out the garbage.
    c. Ann doesn't know what to do with her time.

3. a. at home
    b. in the hospital
    c. in the Center

4. a. sewing
    b. talking with one another
    c. painting

5. a. They are elderly.
    b. They had strokes.
    c. They are becoming forgetful.

6. a. Family members can continue to work.
    b. Family members can have a break.
    c. both a and b

LISTENING DISCRIMINATION

G. Listen and choose. Listen to each sentence. Circle the verb you hear.

1. a. participate   b. participates   c. are participating
2. a. live   b. lives   c. is living
3. a. become   b. becomes   c. is becoming
4. a. work   b. works   c. is working
5. a. follow   b. follows   c. is following

6.	a. come	b. comes		c. are coming
7.	a. offer	b. offers		c. is offering
8.	a. bake	b. bakes		c. are baking
9.	a. learn	b. learns		c. is learning
10.	a. offer	b. offers		c. are offering

H. Listen and write. Listen to each sentence. Write the verb you hear. Some verbs are present tense, some are present continuous.

1. _____   6. _____

2. _____   7. _____

3. _____   8. _____

4. _____   9. _____

5. _____   10. _____

I. Listen and decide. You will hear a statement. Is the grammar correct or incorrect? Circle *correct* or *incorrect*.

1. correct   incorrect   6. correct   incorrect
2. correct   incorrect   7. correct   incorrect
3. correct   incorrect   8. correct   incorrect
4. correct   incorrect   9. correct   incorrect
5. correct   incorrect   10. correct   incorrect

ADULT DAY CARE

J. Cloze. Fill in each blank with the correct word.

David Brown is seventy-two years old. He's friendly and _____ to

talk. He _____ with his wife in a small apartment in the city. But David

_____ _____ forgetful. His wife _____ , "He'll heat

up some soup, then forget to turn off the stove. She is sixty-one and still

_____ . She's worried about leaving her husband alone by himself.

Ann Ramos is eighty and _____ with her daughter, who is sixty. Her

daughter says that she _____ a break. "Mom _____ me

everywhere. She _____ me from room to room when I clean. She

_____ down next to me when I _____ the newspaper.

She even _____ me out of the house when I _____

_____ the garbage. I _____ a break and she

_____ , too."

And so, several times a week, David and Ann's families _____ them

to the Adult Day Care Center. Many hospitals now ___ _____ this program.

Patients _____ to the center for a full or half day, from one to five days a

week. All the patients _____ with their families and most are elderly.

Some _____ _____ forgetful, others _____

_____ from an operation, a stroke, or an accident.

The Center _____ many activities. Patients _____

crafts, such as sewing, woodworking, and painting. Many patients _____

to cook and they _____ fresh bread or other snacks daily. Several men

and women _____ playing checkers, bingo, cards, or other games. All

the patients _____ talking, singing, and being with one another.

Some patients also _____ physical therapy. At Mercy Hospital, one

man _____ _____ to walk with an artificial leg. One woman had a

stroke and cannot move her right arm. She _____ _____ simple

exercises and the movement _____ slowly _____ .

Mrs. Carol Johnson is the director of the center. She states, "We _____

_____ both the patients and their families a valuable service. Patients

_____ to get out of their homes. Husbands, wives or grown children can

work or have a break. Most important, families are able to stay together."

PROBLEMS AT SCHOOL 13

Focus: **Present tense, affirmative and negative**

Discussion: **Discuss these questions with your classmates.**

When you were young, were you ever a problem in class? Did the teacher speak with your mother or father? What did your parents do?

Do you have any children in school? Did you ever receive a note from your child's teacher about his/her behavior? What did you do?

Vocabulary: **Repeat each word after the tape.**

note
widower
neighborhood
behavior

trip
fools around
pay attention
agree

LISTENING COMPREHENSION

A. Fill in. Listen to these sentences. Fill in the new vocabulary words from the list above.

1. He was away for three days on a business _____ .

2. When a student _____ in class, the teacher seats the student alone in a corner.

3. No, he isn't divorced. He's a _____ .

4. Please _____ when I give the directions.

5. If this _____ continues, the teacher is going to call her parents.

6. I _____ with you. He's an excellent student.

7. She lives in a quiet _____ .

8. When a student doesn't do his or her homework, the teacher sends a

_____ to the student's parents.

B. Word association. Circle the two words that you can associate with each new vocabulary word.

1. note   letter, write, quiet
2. widower   man, music, alone
3. neighborhood   area, find, live
4. behavior   conduct, children, necessary
5. trip   go away, year, motel
6. fools around   plays, sleeps, acts stupid
7. pay attention   listen, money, look
8. agree   I don't think so, yes, I think the same

C. First listening. Look at the picture and listen to the conversation. After you listen, tell the class any information you remember about the story.

D. Second listening. Listen to the story again. Then, read these sentences. Who do you think would say each sentence?

         M = Mario   H = Miss Hanson
         T = Mr. Toma   G = Grandmother

_____ 1. I want to play with my friends after school.

_____ 2. Where's your homework?

_____ 3. I don't want Mario to play outside in this neighborhood.

_____ 4. I never left Mario before this.

_____ 5. This new job is difficult for everyone.

_____ 6. Mario, stop talking with John and finish that paper.

_____ 7. Mario is too young to go to the park by himself.

_____ 8. I want to ride my bicycle to my friend's house.

E. Third listening. Read these sentences. Then, listen to the tape a third time. After you listen, write *T* if the statement is true, *F* if the statement is false.

_____   1.   Miss Hanson sent Mr. Toma a note.

_____   2.   Mario is usually a problem at school.

_____   3.   Mario is not doing his work in class.

_____   4.   Mr. Toma is surprised to hear about his son's behavior.

_____   5.   Mr. Toma is away a lot of the time.

_____   6.   Mario likes staying with his grandmother.

_____   7.   Mario has a sister.

_____   8.   Mr. Toma is going to punish Mario.

_____   9.   Mr. Toma is going to call the teacher again next week.

_____ 10.   Miss Hanson is an understanding person.

F. Comprehension questions. Listen to each question. Circle the correct answer.

1.   a. Mario brought home a bad report card.
     b. The teacher called him.
     c. The teacher sent him a note.

2.   a. He completes it.
     b. He sits and looks out the window.
     c. He writes notes.

3.   a. his mother
     b. his grandmother
     c. his aunt

4.   a. His father is away too much.
     b. He doesn't have a mother.
     c. He doesn't like school.

5.   a. his sister
     b. his aunt
     c. his grandmother

6.   a. He should look for a new job.
     b. He should punish Mario.
     c. He should leave Mario with his sister.

LISTENING DISCRIMINATION

G. Listen and choose.   Listen to each sentence. Circle the verb you hear. Several of the verbs are negatives.

1.	a. fool around	b. fools around	c. doesn't fool around
2.	a. pay attention	b. pays attention	c. doesn't pay attention
3.	a. talk	b. talks	c. doesn't talk
4.	a. do	b. does	c. doesn't do
5.	a. look	b. looks	c. doesn't look
6.	a. bring	b. brings	c. doesn't bring
7.	a. know	b. knows	c. don't know
8.	a. understand	b. understands	c. don't understand
9.	a. take	b. takes	c. don't take
10.	a. have	b. has	c. doesn't have

H. Listen and write.   Listen to each sentence. Write the verb you hear. Several of the verbs are negatives.

1. _____   6. _____

2. _____   7. _____

3. _____   8. _____

4. _____   9. _____

5. _____   10. _____

I. Listen and decide.   You will hear a negative statement. Is the grammar correct or incorrect? Circle *correct* or *incorrect.*

1.	correct	incorrect	6.	correct	incorrect
2.	correct	incorrect	7.	correct	incorrect
3.	correct	incorrect	8.	correct	incorrect
4.	correct	incorrect	9.	correct	incorrect
5.	correct	incorrect	10.	correct	incorrect

PROBLEMS AT SCHOOL

J. Cloze.   Fill in each blank with the correct word.

Teacher: Mr. Toma? I'm glad to meet you. I'm Miss Hanson, Mario's teacher.

Parent: Thank you for sending me this note. I'm sorry to hear Mario _____

_____ a problem.

T: I'm not sure what's happening to Mario. He _____ usually an excellent student. He

_____ all his work and he _____ quiet in class. Then, last month, he

just changed.

P: How?

T: Well, he _____ _____ in class. And he _____

_____ _____ . He _____ to the children who sit

near him when he should be reading or writing.

P: Mario? I _____ surprised. What about his work?

T: He _____ _____ it. When I _____ the class to

do an exercise, he _____ and _____ out the window.

Sometimes he _____ pictures on his papers. And he _____

_____ in any homework.

P: I _____ _____ what to say. I _____ _____ what's

happening to him.

T: _____ anything different at home?

P: Well, yes. You _____ that I'm a widower and Mario is my only child. I

_____ a new job and I _____ to take a lot of business

trips. While I'm away, I _____ Mario at his grandmother's.

T: How much _____ you away?

P: Oh, three or four days each week, sometimes five.

T: _____ Mario _____ staying at his grandmother's?

P: Not too much. She _____ old and _____ about him. She

_____ in an apartment building, so he _____ _____ out and

_____ after school. He _____ _____ any friends in her

neighborhood.

A PROFESSIONAL 14

Focus: **Past tense, regular and irregular**

Discussion: **Discuss these questions with your classmates.**

Did a thief ever steal anything from your home or the home of a friend? Tell what happened. Where were you? How did the thief get in? What did the thief take? Did the police catch the thief? How can you protect your home from a thief?

Vocabulary: **Repeat each word after the tape.**

thief	*climbed*
typical	*cash*
briefcase	*silverware*
screwdriver	*touch*

LISTENING COMPREHENSION

A. Fill in. Listen to these sentences. Fill in the new vocabulary words from the list above.

1. The _____ stole their tv and their stereo.

2. Business men and women carry their papers in a _____ .

3. She put together the bicycle with a _____ .

4. I usually take about $100 in _____ with me when I go to the store.

5. Don't _____ the money in my desk. I'm saving it to buy a ring.

6. On a _____ day, I get up at 7:00.

7. Please put the plates and _____ on the table. It's time to eat.

8. The boy _____ up the tree to get into the window on the second floor.

B. Word association.   Circle the two words that you can associate with each new vocabulary word.

1. thief   steal, money, friend
2. typical   regular, letter, average
3. briefcase   papers, short, carry
4. screwdriver   write, turn, open
5. climbed   up and down, sleep, steps
6. cash   car, money, dollar
7. silverware   fork, glass, spoon
8. touch   feel, fingers, goodbye

C. First listening.   Look at the pictures and listen to the story. After you listen, tell the class any information you remember about the story.

D. Second listening.   Listen to the story again. Then, read these sentences. Which picture do they tell about? Write the letter of the correct picture in front of each sentence.

_____ 1. Richard opened the window with a screwdriver.

_____ 2. A man was leaving his house.

_____ 3. Richard found $200 in cash.

_____ 4. Richard began to walk down the street.

_____ 5. At 8:10, he watched a woman leave the same house.

_____ 6. Richard put the silverware into his briefcase.

_____ 7. Richard climbed back out the window.

_____ 8. No one looked at him.

_____ 9. Richard began his walk down the street again.

_____ 10. He stole a diamond ring.

E. Third listening.   Read these sentences. Then, listen to the tape a third time. After you listen, write *T* if the statement is true, *F* if the statement is false.

_____   1.   Richard dressed in a business suit.

_____   2.   Richard parked his car in front of the house he robbed.

_____   3.   Richard saw a man and a woman leave their house together.

_____   4.   No one saw Richard get into the house because he stood behind a tree.

_____   5.   Richard broke the window.

_____   6.   He stole $200 in cash.

_____   7.   He also stole the tv set.

_____   8.   Richard put everything he took into his briefcase.

_____   9.   The police caught Richard when he was in the house.

_____   10.   Richard is an intelligent person.

F. Comprehension questions.   Listen to each question. Circle the correct answer.

1.   a.   because he's a professional
     b.   because he didn't want anyone to look at him.
     c.   because he works hard.

2.   a.   He stood behind a tree.
     b.   He entered the house.
     c.   He walked around the block again.

3.   a.   because it was night time
     b.   because he ran very fast
     c.   because he stood behind a tree

4.   a.   It was too big.
     b.   It was too heavy.
     c.   It was too cold.

5.   a.   five minutes
     b.   fifteen minutes
     c.   one hour

6.   a.   a camera
     b.   a ring
     c.   a stereo

LISTENING DISCRIMINATION

G. Listen and choose.   Listen to each sentence. Circle the verb you hear.

1.	a. think	b. thinks	c. thought
2.	a. has	b. is	c. was
3.	a. take	b. takes	c. took
4.	a. drive	b. drives	c. drove
5.	a. begin	b. begins	c. began
6.	a. see	b. sees	c. saw
7.	a. stand	b. stands	c. stood
8.	a. steal	b. steals	c. stole
9.	a. have	b. has	c. had
10.	a. work	b. works	c. worked

H. Listen and write.   Listen to each sentence. Write the verb you hear.

1. _____   6. _____

2. _____   7. _____

3. _____   8. _____

4. _____   9. _____

5. _____   10. _____

I. Listen and decide.   You will hear a statement in the past tense. Is the grammar correct or incorrect? Circle *correct* or *incorrect*.

1.	correct	incorrect		6.	correct	incorrect
2.	correct	incorrect		7.	correct	incorrect
3.	correct	incorrect		8.	correct	incorrect
4.	correct	incorrect		9.	correct	incorrect
5.	correct	incorrect		10.	correct	incorrect

A PROFESSIONAL

J. Cloze.   Fill in each blank with the correct word.

Richard Williams _____ hard. He's intelligent, careful, and fast. His

work is dangerous. Richard _____ of himself as a professional— a

professional thief.

Yesterday _____ a typical day. Richard dressed in a business suit,

_____ his briefcase, and _____ to a town about ten

miles from home. He _____ his car in a busy area, then

_____ to walk along the street. No one looked at him. He

_____ another businessman, walking to work.

At 8:05, Richard _____ what he wanted. A man was leaving his

house. Richard _____ around the block again. At 8:10, he

_____ a woman leave the same house. After she _____ ,

Richard worked quickly. He _____ to the side of the house and

_____ behind a tree. He _____ a screwdriver out of his

briefcase and quickly _____ the window and _____ in.

First, he _____ through the desk in the living room. He

_____ $200 in cash. In the dining room, he _____ the

silverware into his briefcase. The next stop _____ the bedroom. Richard

_____ a diamond ring and an emerald necklace. Richard passed a color

tv, a stereo, and a camera, but he _____ _____ them. Everything

_____ to fit into his briefcase. In less than five minutes, Richard

_____ back out the window. He looked around carefully, then

_____ his walk down the street again. No one _____ at

him. He _____ just another businessman, walking to work.

MARCO POLO 15

Focus: **Past tense, regular and irregular**

Discussion: **Discuss these questions with your classmates.**

Who was Marco Polo? In what country was he born? Where did he travel? In about what year did he reach China? What did he see there that amazed him?

Vocabulary: **Repeat each word after the tape.**

emperor	amazed
advanced	dictated
descriptions	dug
bark	baths

LISTENING COMPREHENSION

A. Fill in.   Listen to these sentences. Fill in the new vocabulary words from the list above.

1.   Marco Polo _____ his story to a friend. His friend wrote down what he said.

2.   In his _____ , Marco Polo gave the people a picture of what he saw.

3.   In the public _____ , people washed many times a week.

4.   Trees are covered by _____ .

5.   The people _____ into the earth and found black stones.

6.   Marco Polo's stories _____ people. They were surprised to read about a country that was so different.

7.   Kublai Khan was the powerful _____ of China in 1275.

8.   The highways, medicine, and postal system of China were more

_____ than those of Europe.

B. Word association.   Circle the two words that you can associate with each new
vocabulary word.

1.   emperor   leader, king, food
2.   advanced   scared, improved, developed
3.   descriptions   picture, light, story
4.   bark   tree, brown, build
5.   amazed   surprised, unhappy, strange
6.   dictated   wrote, told, made
7.   dug   shovel, music, earth
8.   bath   forget, wash, clean

C. First listening.   Look at the picture and listen to the story. After you listen, tell
the class any information you remember about the story.

D. Second listening.   Read the sentences below. Then, listen to the story again.
Which country does each sentence describe in the year 1275, China or Italy? Write *C*
for China, *I* for Italy.

___C___   1.   People bathed at least three times a week.

_____   2.   People did not bathe very often.

_____   3.   People traveled on paved roads.

_____   4.   People traveled on dirt roads.

_____   5.   People heated their homes with wood.

_____   6.   People heated their homes with coal.

_____   7.   People used gold and silver to buy and sell things.

_____   8.   People used paper money or gold and silver to buy and sell things.

_____   9.   There were crocodiles in the southern areas of this country.

_____ 10.   There were no crocodiles in this country.

E. Third listening.   Read these sentences. Then, listen to the tape a third time. After you listen, write *T* if the statement is true, *F* if the statement is false.

_____ 1. Marco Polo traveled to China alone.

_____ 2. It took over three years to reach China.

_____ 3. Kublai Khan was pleased to have Marco Polo as his guest.

_____ 4. Italy was far more advanced than China.

_____ 5. Marco Polo wrote his book by hand.

_____ 6. The "black stones" that Marco Polo wrote about were really coal.

_____ 7. The highways in China were very beautiful.

_____ 8. Everyone in China had a bath in his or her home.

_____ 9. People in Italy sometimes used paper money.

_____ 10. Marco Polo saw many things that he did not write about.

F. Comprehension questions.   Listen to each question. Circle the correct answer.

1. a. by boat
    b. by horse and camel
    c. by foot
2. a. ten
    b. seventeen
    c. twenty
3. a. by coal
    b. by wood
    c. by electricity
4. a. Europe had paved highways, too.
    b. Europe had dirt roads.
    c. Europe didn't need paved highways.
5. a. an elephant
    b. a tiger
    c. a crocodile
6. a. Yes, everyone did.
    b. No, no one did.
    c. Some people did, others didn't.

LISTENING DISCRIMINATION

G. Listen and choose. Listen to each sentence. Write the regular past verb that you hear.

1. _____   6. _____

2. _____   7. _____

3. _____   8. _____

4. _____   9. _____

5. _____   10. _____

H. Listen and write Listen to each sentence. Write the irregular past verb that you hear.

1. _____   6. _____

2. _____   7. _____

3. _____   8. _____

4. _____   9. _____

5. _____   10. _____

I. Listen and decide. You will hear a statement in the past tense. Is the grammar correct or incorrect? Circle *correct* or *incorrect*.

1. correct   incorrect   6. correct   incorrect
2. correct   incorrect   7. correct   incorrect
3. correct   incorrect   8. correct   incorrect
4. correct   incorrect   9. correct   incorrect
5. correct   incorrect   10. correct   incorrect

MARCO POLO

J. Cloze. Fill in each blank with the correct word.

One of the most famous travelers in all of history _____ Marco Polo. At the age of

seventeen, he _____ Italy with his father and uncle. It _____ them more than three years to cross the mountains and deserts of Asia. In the year 1275, they

_____ the palace of Kublai Khan, the great emperor of China. They

_____ in China for almost twenty years, as guests of the emperor. He

_____ them on many trips around his empire. They _____ amazed at what they

saw. China _____ far more advanced than Europe.

In one area of China, there _____ black stones. People _____ them out of the

mountains. They _____ the black stones and they _____ very slowly,

giving off heat. The people _____ these stones to cook and to heat their homes.

In China there _____ a great system of highways. These highways _____ two

lanes paved with stone or brick. Men _____ trees every ten feet to keep

the sun off of travelers' heads.

The Chinese people _____ also very clean. In every town, there _____ many

public baths. Everyone _____ at least three times a week. Rich families

_____ baths in their homes and _____ daily.

China _____ one of the first countries to use paper money. The government

_____ bills from the bark of a special tree. They _____ the money and

_____ it with the royal seal. The people could use this money the same as

they could use gold or silver.

On one of his trips in the south of China, Marco _____ a strange animal which lived

along the rivers. It _____ like a large piece of wood and _____ more

than ten feet long. Its eyes _____ very large. Its mouth _____ big enough to eat a

man.

Most people _____ Marco Polo's stories. But others _____ him

that they _____ _____ _____ his descriptions. He

_____ that he did not tell half of what he saw.

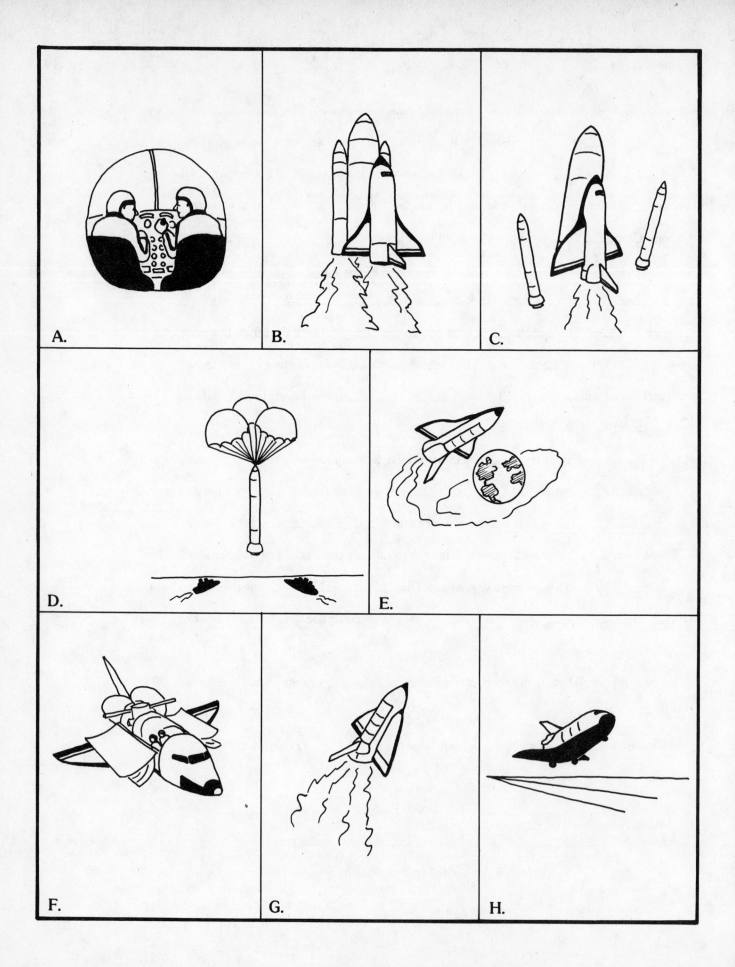

A.

B.

C.

D.

E.

F.

G.

H.

SPACE SHUTTLE   16

Focus: **Past tense**

Discussion: **Discuss these questions with your classmates.**

Did you ever watch the launch of any rocket or space shuttle on television? What was its name? Where was it traveling? What was the reason for the flight? How long did it stay in space? What is a space shuttle?

Vocabulary: **Repeat each word after the tape.**

rocket   astronaut
controls   cargo doors
parachute   space shuttle
orbit   satellites

LISTENING COMPREHENSION

A. Fill in.   Listen to these sentences. Fill in the new vocabulary words from the list above.

1.   A _____ can be used over and over again.

2.   Three to five _____ fly on each space shuttle.

3.   The _____ lifted the space ship into the sky.

4.   John Young, a top pilot, sat at the _____ of Columbia.

5.   The space shuttle can launch satellites through the large_____ .

6.   _____ circle the earth. Some send radio and tv programs from one country to another.

7.   The _____ opened and took the rocket safely down into the ocean.

8.   Columbia circled the earth in an _____ 170 miles high.

B. Word association.   Circle the two words that you can associate with each new vocabulary word.

1. rocket   launch, countdown, receive
2. controls   pilot, quiet, equipment
3. parachute   close, open, umbrella
4. orbit   land, circle, revolve
5. astronaut   space ship, person, robot
6. cargo   carry, transport, automobile
7. space shuttle   separate, vehicle, return
8. satellite   orbit, fired, transmit

C. First listening.   Listen to the story. After you listen, tell the class any information you remember about the story.

D. Second listening.   Listen to the story again. Then, read these sentences from the story. Which pictures do they tell about? Write the number of the correct picture in front of each sentence.

_____ 1.   They opened and closed the cargo doors.

_____ 2.   The booster rockets and the space shuttle separated.

_____ 3.   Ships waited to pick up the booster rockets.

_____ 4.   They made a perfect landing in California.

_____ 5.   John Young and Robert Crippen sat at the controls.

_____ 6.   Young fired the shuttle's engines to slow down the shuttle.

_____ 7.   Columbia climbed to an orbit of 170 miles above earth.

_____ 8.   The space shuttle lifted off into the air.

_____ 9.   Columbia circled the earth thirty-six times.

_____ 10. Parachutes took the booster rockets down into the ocean.

E. Third listening.   Read these sentences. Then, listen to the tape a third time. After you listen, write *T* if the statement is true, *F* if the statement is false.

_____ 1.   A space shuttle can be used many times.

_____ 2.   In the past, spacecraft could only be used two or three times.

_____ 3.   The first space shuttle flight was one week long.

_____ 4. The booster rockets separated from the space shuttle when it was in orbit.

_____ 5. The booster rockets landed in the Pacific Ocean.

_____ 6. The astronauts tested the cargo doors.

_____ 7. Young is an excellent pilot.

_____ 8. Columbia will make many more space flights.

_____ 9. Space shuttles will help scientists learn more about space.

_____ 10. Two space shuttles are now operating.

F. Comprehension questions.   Listen to each question. Circle the correct answer.

1. a. once
    b. twice
    c. many times

2. a. They separated from the space shuttle.
    b. They went into orbit with the space shuttle.
    c. They fell into the ocean.

3. a. twice
    b. 36 times
    c. 170 times

4. a. He fired the engines.
    b. He opened the doors.
    c. He opened the parachutes.

5. a. two
    b. four
    c. sixty

6. a. Astronauts can get into and out of the shuttle.
    b. The booster rockets are inside the doors.
    c. It is easy to launch satellites through the doors.

LISTENING DISCRIMINATION

G. Listen and choose.   Listen to each sentence. Circle the verb you hear.

1. a. travels   b. traveled   c. will travel
2. a. launch   b. launched   c. will launch
3. a. sit   b. sat   c. will sit
4. a. fire   b. fired   c. will fire

5.   a. separate   b. separated   c. will separate
6.   a. circle   b. circled   c. will circle
7.   a. test   b. tested   c. will test
8.   a. enter   b. entered   c. will enter
9.   a. launch   b. launched   c. will launch
10.   a. carry   b. carried   c. will carry

H. Listen and write.   Listen to each sentence. Write the verb you hear.

1. _____   6. _____

2. _____   7. _____

3. _____   8. _____

4. _____   9. _____

5. _____   10. _____

I. Listen and decide.   You will hear a statement in the past time. Is the grammar correct or incorrect? Circle *correct* or *incorrect*.

1.   correct   incorrect   6.   correct   incorrect
2.   correct   incorrect   7.   correct   incorrect
3.   correct   incorrect   8.   correct   incorrect
4.   correct   incorrect   9.   correct   incorrect
5.   correct   incorrect   10. correct   incorrect

SPACE SHUTTLE

J. Cloze.   Fill in each blank with the correct word.

A shuttle is a vehicle that _____ back and forth frequently. A space

shuttle _____ a vehicle, in this case a spacecraft, that _____ into space

and then back again. It can be used again and again. Before this, rockets

_____ all spacecraft. The rocket and the spacecraft could be used only

once.

On April 12, 1981, the United States _____ the first space shuttle,

Columbia. The morning of April 12 _____ clear and sunny. Two astronauts, John

Young and Robert Crippen, _____ at the controls. At 7:00, they _____

the engines. The booster rockets and the space shuttle _____ off into the

air. Two minutes later, 28 miles up, the booster rockets and the space shuttle

_____ . Parachutes _____ the rockets safely down into the Atlantic

Ocean where ships _____ to pick them up. Columbia _____

to climb to an orbit of 170 miles above earth. The space shuttle _____

the earth thirty-six times. During this time, Young and Crippen _____

the equipment on the shuttle. They also _____ and _____

the large cargo doors. Two days later, on April 14, Young _____ the

shuttle's engines. This _____ down the spacecraft. Young, a top pilot,

_____ the controls of Columbia. He _____ the earth's atmosphere

and _____ toward California. At 1:21 p.m., Young _____ a perfect

landing at Edwards Air Force Base.

   Since this first launch, Columbia has traveled into space more than seven times. The

second shuttle, Challenger, _____ also _____ . And the United States

_____ _____ two more space shuttles. It _____

_____ over sixty more shuttle flights. Some _____

_____ satellites through the cargo doors. Some _____ _____ to

manufacture drugs and chemicals in space. One _____ _____ a large

telescope into orbit which _____ _____ pictures back to earth. It is possible that

some day in the future, space shuttles _____ _____ passengers to the

moon.

LOTTERY WINNERS 17

Focus: **Negatives, past and present**

Discussion: **Discuss these questions with your classmates.**

Do you buy lottery tickets? Did you or a friend ever win any money? What did you (or he/she) do with it?
What would you do if you won a million dollars?

Vocabulary: **Repeat each word after the tape.**

- bored
- security
- fault
- opportunity

- spend (time)
- dream
- spent
- quit

LISTENING COMPREHENSION

A. Fill in.   Listen to these sentences. Fill in the new vocabulary words from the list above.

1. I didn't study for the test. If I don't do well, it's my own _____ .

2. My father isn't working now and he doesn't know what to do with his time. He's

   _____ .

3. In the summer, I like to _____ my _____ working in the garden.

4. I _____ of winning a million dollars.

5. As soon as she received her paycheck, she _____ the money for new clothes.

6. Money in the bank brings _____ . You know that if you need it, it's there.

7. After he won the lottery, he _____ his job.

8. She never had the _____ to go to college because she didn't have the time or the money.

B. Word association. Circle the two words that you can associate with each new vocabulary word.

1. bored   not interesting, build, dull
2. security   safe, sure, sleep
3. fault   smoke, responsibility, mistake
4. opportunity   time, mistake, chance
5. spend (time)   use, busy, clock
6. spend   money, buy, throw away
7. dream   tired, look forward to, hope
8. quit   stop, pay for, give up

C. First listening. Look at the picture and listen to the story. After you listen, tell the class any information you remember about the story.

D. Second listening. Listen to the story again. Then, match the person and the information.

_____ Lisa K.
_____ Mark L.
_____ Mabel S.
_____ Jack B.

a. takes interesting vacations
b. is attending art school
c. didn't have enough money for taxes
d. works in the garden
e. didn't like her job
f. didn't quit his job
g. didn't have time for his family
h. paid her son's college tuition

E. Third listening. Read these sentences. Then, listen to the tape a third time. After you listen, write *T* if the statement is true, *F* if the statement is false.

_____ 1. People dream about winning the lottery.

_____ 2. A lottery winner doesn't have to pay taxes.

_____ 3. A person who wins a million dollars receives a check for the total amount.

_____ 4. Lisa K. is now attending art school.

_____ 5. Mark L. doesn't know what to do with all his time.

_____ 6. Mabel S. spent all her money buying things for herself.

_____ 7. Jack B. quit his job.

_____ 8. Jack and his wife bought the house of their dreams.

_____ 9. Jack and his wife don't worry about having money to send their children to college.

_____ 10. Money brings security.

F. Comprehension questions. Listen to each question. Circle the correct answer.

1. a. more than a thousand
   b. more than a hundred thousand
   c. more than a million
2. a. from $25,000 to $40,000
   b. $50,000
   c. a million dollars
3. a. He's working around his house.
   b. He's selling cars again.
   c. He's attending college.
4. a. They bought new homes.
   b. They quit their jobs.
   c. They went back to school.
5. a. She's going to buy another car.
   b. She's going to spend it more carefully.
   c. She's going to save it.
6. a. happiness
   b. good friends
   c. security

LISTENING DISCRIMINATION

G. Listen and choose. Listen to each sentence. Circle the verb you hear. All the verbs are in the negative.

1. a. don't receive	b. doesn't receive	c. didn't receive
2. a. don't have	b. doesn't have	c. didn't have
3. a. don't enjoy	b. doesn't enjoy	c. didn't enjoy
4. a. don't become	b. doesn't become	c. didn't become
5. a. don't want	b. doesn't want	c. didn't want
6. a. don't know	b. doesn't know	c. didn't know

7. a. don't have   b. doesn't have   c. didn't have
8. a. don't quit   b. doesn't quit   c. didn't quit
9. a. don't worry   b. doesn't worry   c. didn't worry
10. a. don't bring   b. doesn't bring   c. didn't bring

H. Listen and write.   Listen to each sentence. Write the verb you hear. All the verbs are in the negative.

1. _____   6. _____

2. _____   7. _____

3. _____   8. _____

4. _____   9. _____

5. _____   10. _____

I. Listen and decide.   You will hear a statement. Is the grammar correct or incorrect? Circle *correct* or *incorrect*. Listen for *don't*, *doesn't*, and *didn't*.

1. correct   incorrect   6. correct   incorrect
2. correct   incorrect   7. correct   incorrect
3. correct   incorrect   8. correct   incorrect
4. correct   incorrect   9. correct   incorrect
5. correct   incorrect   10. correct   incorrect

LOTTERY WINNERS

J. Cloze.   Fill in each blank with the correct word.

Did you ever dream of winning the lottery? So have millions of other people. Every

day, millions of Americans _____ lottery tickets. They _____

_____ to win $50,000, $100,000, one million dollars or more. What

happens after a person wins the lottery?

When a person _____ a million dollars, he _____

_____ a check for the total amount. He _____ $50,000

a year for twenty years. Also, he must pay taxes. After taxes, a million dollar winner

_____ from $25,000 to $40,000 a year for twenty years. This is a lot of

extra spending money.

What have some lottery winners done with their money? Let's look at four past winners.

Lisa K. _____ to be an artist, but she _____ enough money to go to school. She was working at a job she _____ _____. In August, Lisa _____ one ticket and won, two million dollars. She _____ her job three weeks later and _____ now _____ art school. Lisa says, "If I _____ _____ an artist, it's my own fault. I have the opportunity now."

Mark L. _____ a car salesman. He _____ seven days a week and _____ little time for family life. After he won the lottery, he _____ working. Now he _____ his time bowling, working in the garden, and fixing things in his house. But, he's bored. He _____ _____ to sell cars again, but he isn't sure what he wants to do with his life.

Mabel S. was over sixty when she _____ a million dollars. She _____ a new car, new clothes, and new furniture for her house. She _____ for her son's college tuition and bought a car for him, too. Then she _____ all her grandchildren money. After a few months, she _____ no money left to pay her bills. Also, she _____ about her taxes and _____ _____ enough money to pay them. She _____ to spend her money more carefully next year.

Jack B. is one of the small number of winners who _____ _____ his job. Jack still _____ at a nearby school. But, he and his wife now _____ a new car in the garage. They _____ their four children on an interesting vacation every year. And they _____ _____ about sending their children to college. They say that money _____ security and _____ a person opportunities, but it _____ _____ happiness.

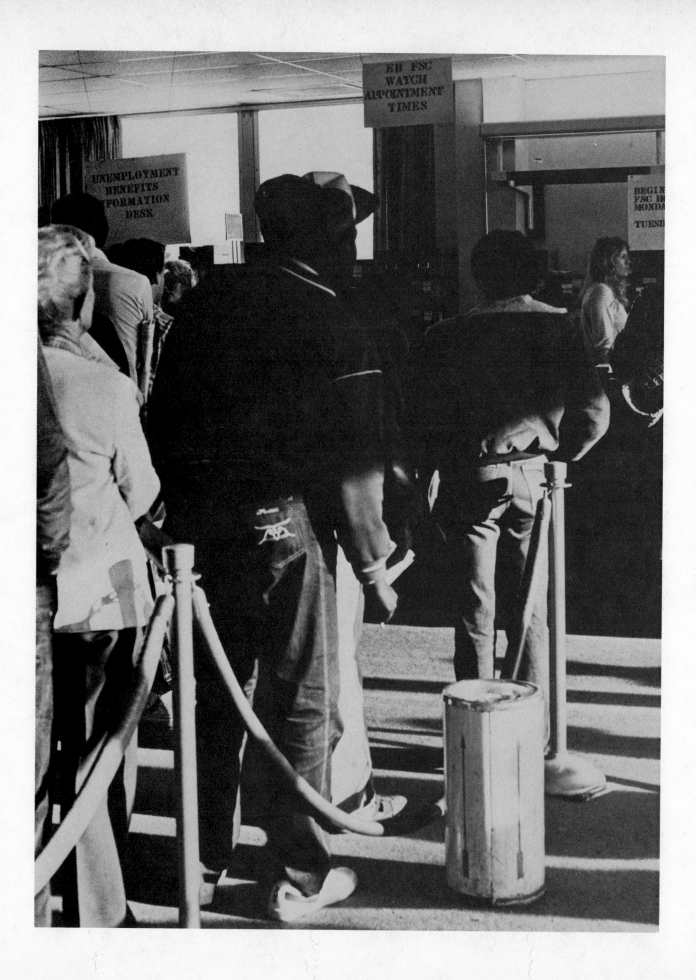

UNEMPLOYMENT   18

Focus: **Past tense**

Discussion: **Discuss these questions with your classmates.**

What are some of the reasons for unemployment? Do you know anyone who is unemployed? Do you know the reason? Did he or she file for unemployment?

Vocabulary: **Repeat each word after the tape.**

interest rate   *is filing a claim*
as a matter of fact   *closed down*
management   *averaged*
luck   *let go*

LISTENING COMPREHENSION

A. Fill in.   Listen to these sentences. Fill in the new vocabulary words from the list above.

1.   Al lost his job. He _____ for unemployment.

2.   Bob got laid off. _____ , all fifty workers at his plant got laid off.

3.   He's having no _____ finding a new job.

4.   People aren't buying as many big cars. One of the big car plants_____

     _____ .

5.   Some months Al sold eight or nine cars, other months he sold eleven or twelve.

     He _____ about ten cars a month.

6.   Very few people are buying cars. The boss_____ three car

     salesmen _____ .

103

7.   The _____ is fourteen percent.

8.   The _____ decided to move the plant from this country to Singapore.

B. Word association.   Circle the two words that you can associate with each new vocabulary word.

1.   interest rates   money, percentage, way
2.   as a matter of fact   really, instead of, actually
3.   management   administration, student, control
4.   luck   enough, chance, fortune
5.   file a claim   fill out papers, buy, information
6.   close down   end, hurry, shut
7.   average   finish, middle, usual
8.   let go   lay off, leave, jail

C. First listening.   Look at the picture and listen to the story. After you listen, tell the class any information you remember about the conversation.

D. Second listening.   In the conversation, the two men talk about several reasons for unemployment. Listen to the conversation again. Check the points below which they include in their conversation.

_____   1.   Labor is cheaper in many other countries.

_____   2.   Workers in the United States don't work hard enough.

_____   3.   Unions often go on strike.

_____   4.   Interest rates are high.

_____   5.   In some plants, the equipment is old.

_____   6.   The United States imports too many items from other countries.

_____   7.   Americans don't save enough money.

_____   8.   Some factory buildings are old.

_____   9.   Taxes are too high.

_____   10.   Many illegal aliens will work for $2.50 an hour.

E. Third listening.   Read these sentences. Then, listen to the tape a third time. After you listen, write *T* if the statement is true, *F* if the statement is false.

_____   1.   The men are in a long line.

_____   2.   The line is usually much shorter.

_____   3.   Al sold ten cars last month.

_____   4.   The interest rates are high.

_____   5.   The workers at the vacuum cleaner plant worked hard.

_____   6.   The company will pay the workers in Singapore less than American workers.

_____   7.   Bob thinks that $2.50 an hour is very low pay.

_____   8.   Bob has been out of work for over a year.

_____   9.   Bob has several job interviews a week.

_____   10.   Al is optimistic that he will find a job soon.

F. Comprehension questions.   Listen to each question. Circle the correct answer.

1.   a.   He's going to file a claim.
     b.   He's going to pick up a check.
     c.   He's going to apply for a job.
2.   a.   People don't save their money.
     b.   Cars are too expensive.
     c.   The interest rates are too high.
3.   a.   because the plant was old
     b.   because the equipment was old
     c.   because labor is much cheaper there
4.   a. $2.50 an hour
     b. $7.00 an hour
     c. $9.00 an hour
5.   a.   Yes, he has one or two interviews a week.
     b.   No, he's happy to have the time off.
     c.   No, he's not looking very hard.
6.   a.   only one or two weeks
     b.   a few months
     c.   ten months or more

LISTENING DISCRIMINATION

G. Listen and choose.   Listen to each sentence. Circle the verb you hear.

1. a. wait   b. waits   c. waited
2. a. sell   b. sells   c. sold
3. a. average   b. averages   c. averaged
4. a. work   b. works   c. worked
5. a. decide   b. decides   c. decided
6. a. make   b. makes   c. made
7. a. close   b. closes   c. closed
8. a. have   b. has   c. had
9. a. like   b. likes   c. liked
10. a. know   b. knows   c. knew

H. Listen and write.   Listen to each sentence. Write the verb you hear.

1. _____   6. _____
2. _____   7. _____
3. _____   8. _____
4. _____   9. _____
5. _____   10. _____

I. Listen and decide.   You will hear a statement in the past tense. Is the grammar correct or incorrect? Circle *correct* or *incorrect*.

1. correct   incorrect   6. correct   incorrect
2. correct   incorrect   7. correct   incorrect
3. correct   incorrect   8. correct   incorrect
4. correct   incorrect   9. correct   incorrect
5. correct   incorrect   10. correct   incorrect

UNEMPLOYMENT

J. Cloze.   Fill in each blank with the correct word.

Al: _____ this the right line to file a claim?

Bob: Yeah. It _____ the same line for everything. You just _____

here and _____ .

Al: Oh. _____ there always such a long line?

Bob: Every week. Sometimes longer. _____ this your first time here?

Al: Yes.

Bob: What _____ ? Your plant close down?

Al: No, I _____ a car salesman, or, I _____ a car salesman. But we just

_____ _____ cars. It _____ the interest rates. Two

years ago, I _____ ten new cars a month. _____ you _____ how

many cars I sold last month? One. One car to a lady who _____ the cash. But the

interest rates _____ up again. The boss _____ three of us _____ . How about

you?

Bob: I _____ at a vacuum cleaner plant with about fifty workers. We

_____ in a good day's work. But the machinery was getting old. As a matter of fact, the

whole plant _____ old. So the management _____ to build a new

plant. You know where? In Singapore. The workers here _____ about seven dollars an

hour, a couple of people _____ eight or nine an hour. You know how much they

_____ _____ the workers in Singapore? $2.50 an hour. Who can live

on $2.50 an hour? Anyway, all fifty of us _____ laid off.

Al: How long ago _____ that?

Bob: They _____ down ten months ago.

Al: Any luck finding another job?

Bob: Nothing. I _____ one, sometimes two, interviews a week. Last week I

_____ I had something. They _____ my experience

with machines. But I never _____ from them again.

Al: At least you _____ something about machines. All I can do is talk.

Bob: Maybe you _____ yourself into another job. Good luck.

I _____ _____ you here next week.

Al: I hope not. I _____ I'll have something by then.

MOUNT ST. HELENS   19

Focus: **Past continuous tense**

Discussion: **Discuss these questions with your classmates.**

What is a volcano? Was there ever a volcanic eruption in your country? If so, give any information you can remember.

Vocabulary: **Repeat each word after the tape.**

volcano   tremors
recreation   eruption
slopes   ash
summit   survived

LISTENING COMPREHENSION

A. Fill in.   Listen to these sentences. Fill in the new vocabulary words from the list above.

1.   The climber placed a flag at the _____ of the mountain.

2.   The _____ of the mountain are covered with snow.

3.   Vesuvius was a _____ that erupted in the year 79 A.D.

4.   _____ shook the earth and the trees.

5.   Only a few people _____ the explosion; most died.

6.   After the fire, the trees were only hot _____ .

7.   The _____ sent rocks and trees into the air.

8.   Yellowstone Park is a _____ area with hiking, camping, swimming, and many other activities.

B. Word association.   Circle the two words that you can associate with each new vocabulary word.

1. volcano   mountain, eruption, decide
2. recreation   play, drive, enjoy
3. slopes   side, climb, throw
4. summit   add, top, high point
5. tremor   noise, shake, soft
6. eruption   face, explosion, volcano
7. ash   smoke, tell, fire
8. survive   die, live, rescued

C. First listening.   Look at the pictures and listen to the story. After you listen, tell the class any information you remember about the story.

D. Second listening.   Read the statements below. Listen to the story again and complete the information as you listen.

1. Mount St. Helens covers _____ square miles.

2. Its last eruption had been _____ years ago.

3. The mountain began to make noises in _____ .

4. Mount St. Helens exploded on _____ .

5. Clouds of dust and ash rose _____ miles into the air.

6. Over _____ people died.

E. Third listening.   Read these sentences. Then, listen to the tape a third time. After you listen, write *T* if the statement is true, *F* if the statement is false.

_____ 1. Most volcanoes erupt every hundred years.

_____ 2. Mount St. Helens gave danger signals before it erupted.

_____ 3. When the volcano began to make noises in March, all the people in the area left immediately.

_____ 4. Mount St. Helens had more power than an atomic bomb.

_____ 5. More than fifty people died when the volcano exploded.

_____ 6. People who lived a hundred miles away could see the clouds of dust and ash.

_____ 7. David Johnston was killed in the explosion.

_____ 8. Robert Barker was near the summit of the mountain when the explosion occurred.

_____ 9. Deer, rabbits, and bears are again living on the mountain.

_____ 10. In the future, Mount St. Helens could erupt again.

F. Comprehension questions. Listen to each question. Circle the correct answer.

1. a. almost every year
    b. every ten years
    c. every hundred years or more
2. a. in 1957
    b. in 1880
    c. in 1857
3. a. morning
    b. afternoon
    c. evening
4. a. noisy
    b. quiet
    c. dark
5. a. He was fishing.
    b. He was camping.
    c. He was standing near the summit.
6. a. a beautiful recreation area
    b. an area of trees and rivers
    c. an empty, gray area

LISTENING DISCRIMINATION

G. Listen and choose. Listen to each sentence. Circle the verb you hear.

1. a. living   b. was living   c. were living
2. a. camping   b. was camping   c. were camping
3. a. fishing   b. was fishing   c. were fishing
4. a. going   b. was going   c. were going
5. a. singing   b. was singing   c. were singing
6. a. moving   b. was moving   c. were moving
7. a. raining   b. was raining   c. were raining
8. a. standing   b. was standing   c. were standing

9. a. camping   b. was camping   c. were camping
10. a. cooking   b. was cooking   c. were cooking

H. Listen and write.   Listen to each sentence. Write the verb you hear.

1. _____   6. _____
2. _____   7. _____
3. _____   8. _____
4. _____   9. _____
5. _____   10. _____

I. Listen and decide.   You will hear a statement in the past continuous tense. Is the grammar correct or incorrect. Circle *correct* or *incorrect*.

1. correct   incorrect   6. correct   incorrect
2. correct   incorrect   7. correct   incorrect
3. correct   incorrect   8. correct   incorrect
4. correct   incorrect   9. correct   incorrect
5. correct   incorrect   10. correct   incorrect

MOUNT ST. HELENS

J. Cloze.   Fill in each blank with the correct word.

Most volcanoes _____ quiet. They _____ peacefully for hundreds of years. No one _____ much attention to them.

Mount St. Helens _____ one of these volcanoes. It's located in the United States in southwest Washington and it _____ over 35 square miles. Until 1980, it _____ a beautiful recreation area. Fishermen _____ large fish in its lakes and rivers, families _____ on its slopes and men and women _____ to its summit. Its last eruption had been 123 years ago. No one _____ worried about another one.

In March 1980, Mount St. Helens _____ to make noises. At first, there _____ tremors. Then, small eruptions _____ .

Some residents _____ immediately. Others felt there _____ no

danger. Nothing _____ _____ to happen.

   But on the morning of May 18, 1980, the mountain _____ its top.

With the power of twenty-five atomic bombs, Mount St. Helens _____ .

Clouds of dust and ash_____ more than twelve miles into the sky. Rocks

and mud _____ down the slopes.

   Unfortunately, many people _____ still _____ ,

_____ , or _____ in the area. Over forty people

_____ their lives. Others were rescued.

   Robert Barker _____ _____ with his family when the explosion

_____ . He_____ that the morning of May 18 _____

strange. No birds _____ . The air _____ still.

Then, he _____ that a large black cloud _____ _____ toward

them. In minutes, day _____ into night. He _____ his

family to their van and they _____ on the slow dark ride away from the

mountain. All the time, hot ash _____ _____ on them.

   But other people _____ not so lucky.

   David Johnston, a volcano expert,_____ _____ near the summit

of the mountain. At 8:31 A.M. he_____ , "This is it!" He was never heard

from again.

   Six friends_____ _____ on the slopes of Mount St. Helens. They

_____ _____ breakfast when they _____ the

explosion and the hot ash _____ to fall on them. Four of them

_____ . The bodies of the other two were found a week later.

THE TITANIC 20

Focus: **Past continuous tense**

Discussion: **Discuss these questions with your classmates.**

What is a disaster? Give a few examples. The Titanic was one of the worst disasters in sea history. Do you know any information about it?

Vocabulary: **Repeat each word after the tape.**

high spirits   panic
luxury   was approaching
iceberg   ripped
lifeboats   sank

LISTENING COMPREHENSION

A. Fill in. Listen to these sentences. Fill in the new vocabulary words from the list above.

1. An _____ is a small or large mountain of ice in the water.

2. After it hit an iceberg, the Titanic _____ to the bottom of the ocean.

3. Every ship carries _____ in case of an accident at sea.

4. The iceberg _____ a large hole in the side of the ship.

5. The icebergs were only a few miles ahead. The ship _____ them at full speed.

6. The passengers were in _____ as their trip began.

7. The _____ ship had a swimming pool, three dining rooms, bars, libraries, and game rooms.

8. As the Titanic sank, people prayed, talked, or held one another. There was no

_____ .

115

B. Word association.   Circle the two words that you can associate with each new vocabulary word.

1. high spirits   happy, airplane, enjoy
2. luxury   comfortable, rich, large
3. iceberg   float, cold, food
4. lifeboat   play, save, emergency
5. panic   sleep, frightened, scream
6. approach   come near, get on, move toward
7. rip   tear, cut, hit
8. sink   water, smell, bottom

C. First listening.   Look at the picture and listen to the story. After you listen, tell the class any information you remember about the story.

D. Second listening.   Read these sentences. Then, listen to the story again. Complete the information as you listen.

1. The Titanic pulled out of port on _____ .

2. She was carrying _____ passengers.

3. The Titanic hit the iceberg on _____ at _____ .

4. The hole in the side of the Titanic was _____ feet long.

5. _____ people lost their lives.

E. Third listening.   Read these sentences. Then, listen to the tape a third time. After you listen, write *T* if the statement is true, *F* if the statement is false.

_____ 1. Arthur Ryerson was a rich man.

_____ 2. Many of the passengers on board the Titanic were wealthy.

_____ 3. The Titanic was traveling across the Pacific.

_____ 4. The Titanic was carrying 2,224 passengers.

_____ 5. No one saw the iceberg before the ship hit it.

_____ 6. The Titanic hit the iceberg around midnight.

_____ 7. The Titanic could not stop in time.

_____ 8. Several people pushed and fought to get a place on a lifeboat.

_____ 9.   Most of the people who died on April 14, 1912 were men.

_____ 10.   Arthur Ryerson was playing cards as the Titanic sank.

F. Comprehension questions.   Listen to each question. Circle the correct answer.

1. a. from New York to England
    b. from England to New York
    c. around the world
2. a. in the south Atlantic
    b. in the middle Atlantic
    c. in the north Atlantic
3. a. drinking
    b. getting ready for bed
    c. playing cards
4. a. one of the crewmen
    b. one of the passengers
    c. Arthur Ryerson
5. a. the crew
    b. women and children
    c. the first passengers to reach them
6. a. He wanted to play cards.
    b. There were not enough lifeboats.
    c. He didn't think the ship was going to sink.

LISTENING DISCRIMINATION

G. Listen and choose.   Listen to each sentence. Circle the verb you hear.

	a.	b.	c.
1.	carried	was carrying	were carrying
2.	enjoyed	was enjoying	were enjoying
3.	knew	was knowing	were knowing
4.	approached	was approaching	were approaching
5.	slept	was sleeping	were sleeping
6.	wrote	was writing	were writing
7.	finished	was finishing	were finishing
8.	stood	was standing	were standing
9.	ripped	was ripping	were ripping
10.	played	was playing	were playing

H. Listen and write.   Listen to each sentence. Write the verb you hear.

1. _____   6. _____

2. _____   7. _____

3. _____   8. _____

4. _____   9. _____

5. _____   10. _____

I. Listen and decide.   You will hear a statement in the past continuous tense. Is the grammar correct or incorrect? Circle *correct* or *incorrect*.

1. correct   incorrect   6. correct   incorrect
2. correct   incorrect   7. correct   incorrect
3. correct   incorrect   8. correct   incorrect
4. correct   incorrect   9. correct   incorrect
5. correct   incorrect   10. correct   incorrect

THE TITANIC

J. Cloze.   Fill in each blank with the correct word.

Millionaire Arthur Ryerson _____ on board the Titanic in high

spirits. He _____ _____ to enjoy this trip across the Atlantic. This

_____ the Titanic's first voyage, a trip from England to New York City. Her decks filled

with libraries, smoking rooms, dining rooms, a gymnasium, and a swimming pool

_____ a relaxing week.

When the Titanic _____ out of port on April 10, 1912, she

_____ _____ 2,224 passengers and crew. The first four days of the

trip _____ clear, calm, and cold. Arthur Ryerson _____ his days

talking, walking, and playing cards with several of his friends. All the passengers

_____ _____ their days aboard the luxury ship. None of them

_____ of the danger ahead. They _____ _____ icebergs.

The evening of April 14 _____ relaxed and friendly. By 11:30, most passengers

_____ _____ or _____ ready for bed. Other

passengers _____ _____ , _____ , or

_____ letters. The band _____ _____ for the

evening. Arthur Ryerson _____ _____ cards with three of his friends.

Out in the cold, one of the crewmen _____ _____ watch.

Suddenly, up ahead, he_____ something in the water. He immediately_____ three

bells and _____ the engine room, "Iceberg, right ahead! Stop!" It

_____ too late. The iceberg _____ a 300-foot hole in the Titanic's

right side. The ship _____ _____ with water and

_____ fast.

There _____ no panic on board. Arthur Ryerson _____ one of the men who

helped women and children into the lifeboats. When he saw there would be no room for

himself or any of the other men on the ship, Ryerson and his three friends

_____ to the smoking room and their game of cards. They_____ still

_____ as the Titanic_____ into the icy waters. On that cold evening in

1912, 1,513 people _____ their lives in one of the worst sea disasters in history.

Focus: **Tense contrast**

Discussion: **Discuss these questions with your classmates.**

Do you know anyone who is hearing impaired? What caused this hearing loss? Does this person wear a hearing aid? How does this person communicate—sign language, speaking, lip reading?

Vocabulary: **Repeat each word after the tape.**

increase	*results*
dependent	*approach*
impaired	*therapist*
senses	*skill*

LISTENING COMPREHENSION

A. Fill in.   Listen to these sentences. Fill in the new words from the list above.

1.   We have five _____: hearing, smelling, touch, taste, and sight.

2.   Listening is not a sense; it's a ____ Skill ____. We must learn it.

3.   A person who cannot hear well is called hearing ____ impaired ____.

4.   The _____ of the hearing test showed that Vicki was almost deaf.

5.   A speech _____ is a teacher who helps people to learn to speak.

6.   We wanted Vicki to learn to listen, we didn't want her to be

_____ on speaking with her hands.

7. We didn't want Vicki to speak with her hands. We wanted a different

_____ .

8. The children played games to _____ their listening skills.

B. Word association.   Circle the two words that you can associate with each new vocabulary word.

1. increase   improve, better, hurt
2. dependent   limited, receive, subject to
3. impaired   two, injured, hurt
4. sense   feeling, sight, size
5. results   test, answers, active
6. approach   method, stand, program
7. therapist   teacher, help, typist
8. skill   learn, practice, believe

C. First listening.   Look at the pictures and listen to the story. After you listen, tell the class any information you remember about the story.

D. Second listening.   Read these sentences. Then, listen to the story again. Check the statements that Vicki's parents would agree with.

_____ 1. If your child needs special help, start her or him with a special program when he or she is very young.

___a___ 2. Look at several programs before you decide what's right for your child.

__dis__ 3. A hearing impaired child needs no special help.

___a___ 4. Parents can do a lot to help at home.

___d___ 5. The school system always knows what is best for your child.

___a___ 6. Parents should do all that they can for their children.

___a___ 7. Signing is the wrong approach for all children.

___a___ 8. It's important to remember that children need to play and have fun.

___a___ 9. A special child will need extra time from his or her parents.

_____ 10. Wait until your child goes to kindergarten to see if she or he needs special classes.

E. Third listening.   Read these sentences. Then, listen to the tape a third time. After you listen, write *T* if the statement is true, *F* if the statement is false.

_____   1.   Vicki was a slow child.

__T___   2.   Vicki is profoundly deaf.

_____   3.   With a hearing aid, Vicki can hear everything.

_F T__   4.   Vicki started in special school when she was two years old.

_____   5.   The school made learning fun.

_____   6.   The therapist practices listening and speech with Vicki.

__✓___   7.   Vicki goes to a school for hearing impaired children.

_____   8.   Vicki can hear the children in her class when they talk.

_____   9.   Vicki's speech is now perfect.

_____ 10.   Vicki feels good about herself.

F. Comprehension questions.   Listen to each question. Circle the correct answer.

1.   a. only a few months old
     b. two years old
     c. four years old

2.   a. talking with your hands
     b. lip reading
     c. listening very carefully

3.   a. signing
     b. playing games
     c. listening and speaking

4.   a. They told her stories.
     b. They helped her learn new words.
     c. They taught her sounds.

5.   a. to practice sounds
     b. to teach her verb tenses
     c. to increase her listening ability

6.   a. a school for hearing impaired children
     b. a regular school
     c. a therapist

LISTENING DISCRIMINATION

G. Listen and choose.   Listen to each sentence. Circle the verb you hear.

1. a. is walking   b. walks   c. walked
2. a. are waiting   b. wait   c. waited
3. a. are learning   b. learn   c. learned
4. a. are playing   b. play   c. played
5. a. is entering   b. enters   c. entered
6. a. is wearing   b. wears   c. wore
7. a. is carrying   b. carries   c. carried
8. a. is doing   b. does   c. did
9. a. is improving   b. improves   c. improved
10. a. is liking   b. likes   c. liked

H. Listen and write.   Listen to each sentence. Write the verb you hear.

1. _____   6. _____

2. _____   7. _____

3. _____   8. _____

4. _____   9. _____

5. _____   10. _____

VICKI

I. Cloze.   Fill in each blank with the correct word.

We _____ we had to begin early to help Vicki with her hearing and speech. We

_____ _____ to wait until she began school. So we

_____ into several programs. In one school, the children

_____ signing; that is, how to talk with their hands. But we _____

worried that she would become too dependent on signing and not learn to listen or speak.

We _____ a different approach. We _____ Vicki in a special school for

hearing impaired children. The school _____ listening, speaking, and

lip reading. The school _____ that hearing is a sense; listening is a skill

that must be learned. The children _____ games to increase their listening ability. In one game, each child _____ a box and a few blocks. Then the

teacher _____ a story. Whenever the children _____ a certain word,

they _____ a block into the box. We _____ with Vicki at

home, too. We _____ her the names of everything in the house. We

_____ things with Vicki and carefully _____ every action.

Vicki _____ to speak when she _____ three years old. At four, she

_____ _____ more, but we _____

_____ what she _____ _____ . She

_____ lessons with a speech therapist. The therapist

_____ her listening even more. Vicki _____ , then

_____ directions with blocks, toys and other objects. The therapist _____

a picture. Vicki _____ , then _____ to the part the

therapist _____ _____ . Vicki _____ her speaking,

beginning with basic sounds.

When she _____ five, Vicki _____ kindergarten in a regular

public school. She _____ a second grader there now. Vicki _____ the only hearing

impaired child in the school. In class, she _____ an auditory trainer. This

_____ a special hearing aid. The teacher _____ a microphone on her

clothes and Vicki _____ the receiver in her pocket. Vicki

_____ only what the teacher says, not other noises, such as doors

opening and closing and cars passing by. Vicki also _____ with a speech

teacher one hour a day. Vicki _____ _____ very well in school.

After school and speech lessons, it _____ time to get down to the business of being

a normal seven year old. Vicki _____ to play with her friends, ride her

bicycle, and go to the park. She _____ to friends that she _____

_____ how to swim and can jump off the high dive. Vicki _____ proud

of herself and we _____ proud of her, too.

Focus: Tense contrast

Discussion: **Discuss these questions with your classmates.**

What country are you from? What year did you leave your country? Did all of your family come to this country, or did some members stay? Why did you leave? What was the most difficult part of your first year here? What are some of your goals for the future?

Vocabulary: **Repeat each word after the tape.**

civil war	standards
massacre	settled
graves	bound
alternatives	fled

LISTENING COMPREHENSION

A. Fill in.   Listen to these sentences. Fill in the new vocabulary words from the list above.

1. The ship was _____ for the United States.

2. During the _____ , the soldiers killed all the residents of the town.

3. The students dug _____ for the people who had been killed in the massacre.

4. When they heard that the soldiers were marching toward the city, the residents

   _____ .

5. In the _____ , the North was fighting the South.

6. After he went to live with a friend, Vi felt more _____ .

7. Vi's family escaped to Saigon. What were the _____ after that?

8. Vi set high _____ for his life.

B. Word association.   Circle the two words that you can associate with each new vocabulary word.

1. civil war   national war, world-wide war, internal war
2. massacre   killing, peace, murder
3. graves   serious, funeral, burial
4. alternative   choice, decision, change
5. standard   ideal, value, part
6. settled   start, relaxed, secure
7. bound   headed, pleased, direction
8. fled   escaped, ran, plan

C. First listening.   Look at the picture and listen to the story. After you listen, tell the class any information you remember about the story.

D. Second listening.   Read the statements below. Then listen to the story again. About when did each event happen? Write the letter of the correct time in front of each sentence.

C = When Vi was a *child*   YM = When Vi was a *young man*
HS = When Vi was in *high school*   US = After Vi came to the *United States*

_____   1. Vi helped to gather supplies for a bombed village.

_____   2. Towns in South Vietnam were falling to the North Vietnamese.

_____   3. Vi graduated with a B.S. in engineering.

_____   4. The war didn't affect his town or his family.

_____   5. Vi and his family fled to the capital, Saigon.

_____   6. Vi began to hear bombings and saw rockets in the sky.

_____   7. Vi went from job to job, from sponsor to sponsor.

_____   8. Vi got in line with hundreds of other Vietnamese.

_____   9. Vi decided to go to college.

_____ 10. A civil war was already ongoing in Vietnam.

E. Third listening.   Read these sentences. Then, listen to the tape a third time. After you listen, write *T* if the statement is true, *F* if the statement is false.

_____   1.   In Vietnam, the North was fighting the South.

_____   2.   When Vi was young, there was fighting in his town.

_____   3.   As a high school student, Vi saw the effects of war.

_____   4.   The United States helped South Vietnam in the war.

_____   5.   Vi's family lost their house and business.

_____   6.   Vi and his family left Vietnam together.

_____   7.   Vi entered the United States as a political refugee.

_____   8.   Vi lived in several different places during his first year in the United States.

_____   9.   Vi immediately felt comfortable in the American culture.

_____ 10.   Vi is completely satisfied with his life now.

F. Comprehension questions.   Listen to each question. Circle the correct answer.

1.   a.   North Vietnam was fighting South Vietnam.
   b.   The United States was fighting North Vietnam.
   c.   The United States was fighting South Vietnam.

2.   a.   Bombs fell near Vi's home.
   b.   The North Vietnamese were marching toward Vi's home.
   c.   Vi was more affected by the war.

3.   a.   because his family lost their business
   b.   because he wanted to go to college
   c.   because the political situation was so unsettled

4.   a.   He moved from place to place, from job to job.
   b.   He took a job in an engineering firm.
   c.   He went to college.

5.   a.   He borrowed the money from his friend.
   b.   He worked two different jobs.
   c.   He saved the money before he went.

6.   a.   the language
   b.   the culture
   c.   the weather

LISTENING DISCRIMINATION

G. Listen and choose.   Listen to each sentence. Circle the verb you hear.

1. a. fit   b. fitted   c. were fitting
2. a. becomes   b. became   c. was becoming
3. a. gather   b. gathered   c. were gathering
4. a. loses   b. lost   c. was losing
5. a. fall   b. fell   c. were falling
6. a. remain   b. remained   c. were remaining
7. a. borrows   b. borrowed   c. were borrowing
8. a. works   b. worked   c. was working
9. a. thinks   b. thought   c. was thinking
10. a. hopes   b. hoped   c. was hoping

H. Listen and write.   Listen to each sentence. Write the verb you hear.

1. _____   6. _____

2. _____   7. _____

3. _____   8. _____

4. _____   9. _____

5. _____   10. _____

VI

I. Cloze.   Fill in each blank with the correct word.

By 1974, the fighting _____ much more serious. The United States _____

_____ with the South Vietnamese against the North. But the South

_____ _____ . Towns in South Vietnam _____

_____ to the North Vietnamese. Vi _____ now back home with his

family. But DaNang _____ no longer safe. Vi and his family _____ at night to the

capital, Saigon, leaving their home, business, and belongings.

Vi and his family _____ in Saigon for many months. They constantly

_____ the alternatives. Should they go back to DaNang? Should they try to leave the country? Should they stay in Saigon? The North Vietnamese army

_____ _____ toward the capital. Vi, now twenty years old,

_____ to leave. His family _____ . At the United States

embassy, Vi _____ in line with hundreds of other Vietnamese. A bus _____ him and

many others to the airport. A helicopter _____ them out of Vietnam and onto a waiting

United States ship. Vi _____ now a political refugee, bound for the United States.

"My first year in the United States _____ crazy," comments Vi. "I _____ in Fort

Chaffee in Arkansas, Oklahoma, then Texas. I _____ several different sponsors. I

_____ _____ where I wanted to go or what I wanted to do." Vi

_____ three different jobs. In the evenings, he _____ English at

different adult schools.

Finally, in 1977, a friend _____ him to come to live in New Jersey. Vi

_____ . His life _____ more settled and he

_____ to enter college. In order to attend, Vi _____ two part-time jobs

and _____ money from the government. In 1981, he

_____ with a B.S. in industrial engineering. Vi states that he _____

_____ too much trouble with English in college. He adds that it was five

times more difficult to understand the culture and feel comfortable with people.

Vi now _____ as a design engineer for a consulting firm. He

_____ heating, ventilating and air conditioning systems. Vi is not

satisfied with being "average." He says, "I wanted a job and standards that I would be

satisfied with." Vi _____ still _____ to school. Sometimes he

_____ of going to law school, other times he _____ the

idea of having his own engineering firm. Or, maybe he _____

_____ . As he _____ into the future, Vi

_____ for a strong marriage, a good family, and a comfortable life in a

small town.

TAPESCRIPTS

1. Apartment Problems

A. Fill in. Listen to these sentences. Fill in the new vocabulary words from the list above.
1. I can't open the door. It's stuck.
2. It's cold in this room. The radiator isn't turned on.
3. They don't have any children. They're expecting their first child next month.
4. The pipe in the sink is stopped up. Water is overflowing onto the floor.
5. Our apartment is small, there are only a few rooms.
6. The refrigerator doesn't work. The landlord is going to fix it.
7. There's a problem in the bathroom upstairs. The water is leaking through the ceiling into the living room.
8. Nothing is clean and food and clothes are all over. This place is a mess.

STORY—UNIT 1—Apartment Problems

Theresa and Charles live in Chicago. They rent a one-bedroom apartment. Theresa is expecting a baby in two months, so they're looking for a larger apartment.

Theresa and Charles are talking to the landlord in a large apartment building. He's showing them an apartment in his building. A family is living there now, but they're going to move next week. The landlord is also saying that there are a few problems in the apartment, but he's going to fix them.

Theresa and Charles are looking around the apartment. They can't believe the mess! In the kitchen, the oven door is open and the oven is smoking. Theresa is trying to open the refrigerator, but she can't. The door is stuck. And the heat isn't working, no hot air is coming up from the radiator.

Charles is in the bathroom. He can't see too well because the light isn't working. The sink is overflowing. Water is going all over the floor and Charles can't turn it off. And water is leaking from the ceiling. There's probably a problem in the apartment above this one.

Theresa and Charles aren't going to rent this apartment. They're leaving in a hurry!

F. Comprehension questions. Listen to each question. Circle the correct answer.
1. How many bedrooms do Theresa and Charles have in their apartment now?
2. When is the family who is living in the apartment now going to move?
3. Why can't Theresa open the refrigerator door?
4. Why can't Charles see in the bathroom?
5. Why is water leaking from the ceiling?
6. Why is the apartment a mess?

G. Listen and choose. Listen to each sentence. Circle the verb you hear.
1. Theresa is expecting a baby.
2. They're looking for a larger apartment.
3. Theresa and Charles are talking to the landlord.
4. A family is living here now.
5. The oven is smoking.
6. The heat isn't working.
7. No hot air is coming up from the radiator.
8. The sink is overflowing.
9. Water is leaking from the ceiling.
10. They're leaving in a hurry.

H. Listen and write. Listen to each sentence. Write the verb you hear.
1. Theresa is expecting a baby in two months.
2. They're looking around an apartment.
3. The landlord is showing them the apartment.
4. He's telling them about a few problems.
5. Theresa is trying to open the refrigerator.
6. No hot air is coming up from the radiator.
7. The sink is overflowing.
8. Water is going all over the floor.
9. Water is leaking from the ceiling.
10. They're leaving in a hurry.

I. Listen and decide. You will hear a statement in the present continuous tense. Is the grammar correct or incorrect? Circle *correct* or *incorrect*.
1. Theresa is expecting a baby.
2. They looking for an apartment.
3. They're talk to the landlord.
4. A family living here now.
5. Theresa and Charles are look around the apartment.
6. No hot air is coming up from the radiator.
7. The sink is overflowing.
8. Water go all over the floor.
9. Water leaking from the ceiling.
10. They're leaving in a hurry.

2. The Magician

A. Fill in. Listen to these sentences. Fill in the new vocabulary words from the list above.
1. The audience is sitting in the theater and watching the magician.
2. The magician is standing on the stage so that everyone can see him.

3. The man is sawing the tree in half.
4. I don't understand how the magician can do those tricks.
5. The woman is climbing into the large, empty box.
6. The magician is wearing a tall black hat and a black coat.
7. It looks like the magician is sawing her in half, but she's really in one piece.
8. The magician is asking for someone to help him. He needs a volunteer.

STORY—UNIT 2—The Magician

Bart is a magician. People love to watch him do tricks, but they never understand how he does them. These are two of his favorites.

First, the rabbit trick. According to Bart, this one is simple. In picture A, Bart is standing in back of a table. The table is flat; there's nothing on it or under it. In picture B, Bart is taking off his hat and showing the audience that there's nothing inside it. He's putting the hat on the table. Next, Bart is pulling a rabbit out of his hat. Not just one rabbit, five of them! The rabbits are hopping all over the stage. Finally, in the last picture, Bart is putting his hat back on his head again.

Another trick that Bart enjoys is the box trick. This one is much more difficult. In picture E, Bart is showing the audience a large, empty box. He's also asking for a volunteer to come up on stage. In picture F, a young woman is climbing into the box. We can see her head on one end, her feet on the other. Next, Bart is sawing the box in half! He's sawing the box from top to bottom. In picture H, he's pulling the box apart. The young woman's head is on the left of the stage, her feet are on the right. In picture I, Bart is pushing the box back together again. And, finally, the young woman is climbing out of the box again, all in one piece.

F. Comprehension questions. Listen to each question. Circle the correct answer.
1. Why do people like to watch magicians?
2. Why is the table flat?
3. Where were the rabbits that Bart took out of his hat?
4. What does Bart want the volunteer to do?
5. What is Bart really doing in the second trick?
6. According to Bart, which trick is simple?

G. Listen and choose. Listen to each sentence. Circle the preposition you hear.
1. Bart is standing in back of a table.
2. There's nothing on it.
3. There's nothing under it.
4. There's nothing inside his hat.
5. A young woman is coming up on the stage.
6. A young woman is climbing into the box.
7. We can see her head on one end.
8. Bart is sawing the box in half.
9. He's sawing the box from top to bottom.
10. The woman is all in one piece.

H. Listen and write. Listen to each sentence. Write the preposition you hear.
1. Bart is standing in back of a table.
2. He's putting the hat on the table.
3. There's nothing inside his hat.
4. A young woman is coming up on the stage.
5. She's climbing into the box.
6. Her feet are on one end.

7. Bart is sawing the box in half.
8. Her head is on the left.
9. Finally, she's climbing out of the box.
10. She's in one piece.

I. Listen and decide. You will hear a statement with a preposition of place. Is the preposition correct or incorrect? Circle *correct* or *incorrect*.
1. Bart is standing back of the box.
2. There's nothing in the table.
3. He's putting the hat into the table.
4. Bart is putting his hat back on his head.
5. Bart is asking for a volunteer to come up under the stage.
6. A young woman is climbing into the box.
7. Bart is sawing the box from top in bottom.
8. The young woman's head is in the left.
9. Finally, the woman is climbing out the box.
10. She's all in one piece.

3. The Census

A. Fill in. Listen to these sentences. Fill in the new vocabulary words from the list above.
1. The population of the United States is about 226 million people.
2. A census counts the number of people who live in a country.
3. How many residents live in this country?
4. How often does the United States conduct a census?
5. The population of the United States is growing larger.
6. Many people are choosing to move to a warmer climate.
7. Cars, factories, and noise cause pollution.
8. The population of Pennsylvania is declining because many factories have closed.

STORY—UNIT 3—The Census

Every ten years the United States conducts a census of the population. A census is a count of the people who live in a city or country. Every family receives a form with questions about family size, income, jobs, etc. They answer questions such as: How many people are in your family? Do you live in a house or in an apartment? How long have you been living there? Where did you live before this? Where do you work? How much money do you make? The government uses this information to get a better picture of its residents.

The last census was in 1980. The population of the United States is now 226,500,000. The population is up 23 million people from 1970. In 1970, the population was 203,000,000.

The census shows that some areas of the United States are declining in population while other areas are growing. In the past, more people lived in the Northeast and North Central areas. But this is changing. Now, more people live in the South than in any other area. People are moving from the North to the South and the West. The population of northern cities is down from 1970. For example, the population of New York City is down 11%, the population of Chicago is down 12%. In Pennsylvania, the population of Philadelphia is down 14% and the population of Pittsburgh is down 18%. Washington, D.C. has almost 16% less people. At the same time that northern cities are declining, southern and western cities are growing. The population of San Jose is up 24%. Phoenix is up

33%. In Texas, Houston is up 26% and El Paso is up 31%. In Florida, the population of Ft. Lauderdale is up 10%. The population of Virginia Beach is up 52%.

Why are people leaving the North? Why are they moving to the South and West? The number one reason is jobs. Because the South and West are growing, there's a need for builders, teachers, salespeople, etc. People still want to live in cities, but they are choosing smaller cities. They're tired of crime, traffic, and pollution. Finally, people say they are looking for a warmer climate. They are moving away from the cold, toward the sun.

F. Comprehension questions. Listen to each question. Circle the correct answer.
1. How often does the United States government conduct a census?
2. Which of these questions would be on a census form?
3. In which city is the population growing?
4. How are people moving?
5. What is one reason that people are moving South and West?
6. When will the government conduct the next census?

G. Listen and choose. Listen to each sentence. Circle the verb you hear.
1. The population of New York City is declining.
2. The population of Houston is growing.
3. How many people are in your family?
4. Some areas of the United States are growing in population.
5. This is changing.
6. People are moving from the North to the South and the West.
7. In some areas, the population is declining.
8. Why are poeple leaving the North?
9. They're looking for a warmer climate.
10. People are choosing to live in smaller cities.

H. Listen and write. Listen to each sentence. Write the verb you hear.
1. The population in Washington, D.C. is declining.
2. The population in San Jose is growing.
3. People are moving from the North to the South.
4. Southern and western cities are growing.
5. The population in other areas is declining.
6. Why are people moving?
7. The number one reason is jobs.
8. They're choosing smaller cities.
9. They're looking for a warmer climate.
10. They're moving toward the sun.

I. Listen and decide. You will hear a statement in the present continuous tense. Is the grammar correct or incorrect? Circle *correct* or *incorrect*.
1. Some areas of the United States are growing.
2. Other areas declining.
3. This is changing.
4. People are move.
5. People leaving the North.
6. They are moving to the South.
7. The South and the West growing.
8. People are looking for a warmer climate.
9. They're move away from the cold.
10. They choosing smaller cities.

4. Back in Town

A. Fill in. Listen to these sentences. Fill in the new vocabulary words from the list above.
1. How come you're working late tonight?
2. He's retiring after working at the company for 40 years.
3. I work in New York. My company is transferring me to Chicago.
4. The new plant is going to make computer parts.
5. She doesn't have a boyfriend. She isn't dating anyone.
6. He's looking forward to his vacation next month.
7. He's managing a store in Texas. He's the boss.
8. I'm living in Florida now. So is my sister.

STORY—UNIT 4—Back in Town

George: Sarah! Is that you?
Sarah: George?
George: Yes! It's been three years!
Sarah: Yes, since you left for Texas.
George: How are you? You look great!
Sarah: Thanks. So do you.
George: What are you doing now?
Sarah: I'm working for a small company in town. I'm a bookkeeper.
George: And how's Paul?
Sarah: Paul! We're not dating anymore. Not for years.
George: I'm surprised to hear that.
Sarah: How about you? How come you're back in town?
George: I'm visiting my parents. My father is retiring and his company is giving him a retirement party.
Sarah: That's great. Are you still working for Disk Computers?
George: Yes. Right now I'm living in Texas, but they are transferring me back to Florida again soon. They're opening a new plant in Miami and I'm going to manage it.
Sarah: I'm sure your parents are happy that you're returning.
George: Yes, and I'm looking forward to coming back again, too. Can I call you next month when I return?
Sarah: Of course! I'd like that. Have a wonderful time at your father's party.
George: Thanks. Goodbye Sarah.
Sarah: Bye, George.

F. Comprehension questions. Listen to each question. Circle the correct answer.
1. Where is George living now?
2. Why is George back in town?
3. Who is Paul?
4. Where are George and Sarah now?
5. What is George surprised about?
6. What is going to happen when George returns to Florida next month?

G. Listen and choose. Listen to each sentence. Circle the verb you hear.
1. I'm working for a small company in town.
2. What are you doing now?
3. We're not dating anymore.
4. I'm visiting my parents.
5. My father is retiring.
6. His company is giving him a retirement party.

7. Are you still working for Disk Computers?
8. I'm living in Texas.
9. They are transferring me back to Florida.
10. I'm looking forward to it.

H. Listen and write. Listen to each sentence. Write the verb you hear.
1. I'm working for a small company in town.
2. We're not dating anymore.
3. I'm visiting my parents.
4. My father is retiring.
5. I'm living in Texas.
6. They're opening a new plant in Miami.
7. I'm looking forward to it.
8. They're transferring me back to Florida.
9. Are you still working for Disk Computers?
10. His company is giving him a retirement dinner.

H. Listen and decide. You will hear a statement in the present continuous. Is the grammar correct or incorrect? Circle *correct* or *incorrect*.
1. They're open a new plant in Miami.
2. His company is giving him a retirement dinner.
3. Are you still date Paul?
4. I visiting my parents.
5. I'm living in Texas.
6. My father retiring.
7. I'm looking forward to it.
8. Are you still working for Disk Computers?
9. I working for a small company in town.
10. They are transferring me back to Florida.

5. The Experiment

A. Fill in. Listen to these sentences. Fill in the new vocabulary words from the list above.
1. Scientists are experimenting with animals.
2. They have a good diet with fruit, vegetables, bread, milk, and meat.
3. His health is excellent. He's never sick.
4. Monkeys are active animals. They're always jumping, running, and playing.
5. A scientist usually works in a laboratory.
6. The experiment is ongoing. It isn't finished yet.
7. Ten cups of food is a large amount to eat.
8. What is the relationship between smoking and health?

STORY—UNIT 5—The Experiment

One way that scientists learn about man is by studying animals, such as mice, rats, and monkeys. The scientists in this laboratory are experimenting on mice. They are studying the relationship between diet and health. At this time, over one hundred experiments are ongoing in this laboratory.

In this experiment, the scientists are studying the relationship between the amount of food the mice eat and their health. The mice are in three groups. All three groups are receiving the same healthy diet. But the amount of food that each group is receiving is different. The first group is eating one cup of food each day, the second group is eating two cups, and the third group of mice is eating three cups.

After three years, the healthiest group is the one that is only eating one cup of food each day. The mice in this group are thinner than normal mice. But they are more active. Most of the day, they are running, playing with one another, and using the equipment in their cages. Also, they are living longer. Mice usually live for two years. Most of the mice in this group are still alive after three years.

The second group of mice is normal weight. They are healthy, too. They are active, but not as active as the thinner mice. But they are only living about two years, not the three years or more of the thinner mice.

The last group of mice is receiving more food than the other two groups. Most of the day, these mice are eating or sleeping. They're not very active. These mice are living longer than the scientists thought—about a year and a half. But they aren't as healthy. They're sick more often than the other two groups.

The experiment is still ongoing. The scientists hope to finish their studies in two years.

F. Comprehension questions. Listen to each question. Circle the correct answer.
1. What are the scientists in this laboratory studying?
2. Which group is receiving the most food?
3. Why is the first group the thinnest?
4. How long do normal mice live?
5. Which group is the healthiest?
6. What is one possible relationship between the diet of mice and the diet of people?

G. Listen and choose. Listen to each sentence. Circle the verb you hear.
1. Scientists learn about man by studying animals.
2. The scientists in this laboratory are experimenting with mice.
3. They are studying the relationship between diet and health.
4. Over one hundred experiments are ongoing.
5. The amount of food each group is receiving is different.
6. The first group is eating one cup of food each day.
7. They are playing with one another.
8. They are using the equipment in their cages.
9. Mice usually live for two years.
10. These mice are sleeping most of the day.

H. Listen and write. Listen to each sentence. Write the verb you hear.
1. The scientists are experimenting on mice.
2. They are studying the relationship between diet and health.
3. Many experiments are ongoing in the laboratory.
4. The first group is receiving one cup of food each day.
5. The second group is eating two cups of food per day.
6. The mice in the first group are playing most of the day.
7. They are living three years or more.
8. The mice in the third group are sleeping most of the day.
9. This third group is living about a year and a half.
10. The experiment is still ongoing.

I. Listen and decide. You will hear a statement in the present continuous tense. Is the grammar correct or incorrect? Circle *correct* or *incorrect.*
1. The scientists in this laboratory are experimenting on mice.
2. They are study the relationship between diet and health.
3. Over one hundred experiments are ongoing.
4. All three groups receiving the same healthy diet.
5. The amount each group is receive is different.
6. The third group eating three cups of food each day.
7. The mice in the first group are playing most of the day.
8. They are live longer.
9. Most of the day, the mice in the third group sleeping.
10. This group is living about a year and a half.

6. Robots

A. Fill in. Listen to these sentences. Fill in the new vocabulary words from the list above.
1. The workers will go on strike for higher pay.
2. Robots can't walk, they roll around on wheels.
3. If a robot breaks down, we will call a mechanic.
4. It is difficult to support a family on $200 a week.
5. What's in this cough syrup? Read the ingredients on the label.
6. Mix the ingredients together for five minutes.
7. Measure the exact amount, not too much, not too little.
8. Can a robot pour the syrup into the bottles carefully?

STORY—UNIT 6—Robots

Boss: Robots? Why are you talking about robots? We're a small company, we make cough syrup. We only have twenty workers. Robots are fine for large factories, not small ones like ours.
Assistant: Boss, small companies can use robots, too. They're great workers.
Boss: I don't know. Talk to me about them ten years from now.
Assistant: Boss, listen, this is a simple operation here. We make ten different kinds of cough syrup. But each operation only has five steps, so we'll only need five robots. One robot will measure the ingredients, and a second robot will mix them. A third robot will pour the syrup into the bottles. Then a fourth robot will put on the labels. The last robot will pack the bottles into boxes. Right now, we have twenty workers doing those jobs.
Boss: But each kind of syrup is different. How will these robots know what to do?
Assistant: We'll tell them. One worker will program the robots. She'll just type the orders into a computer. She'll tell the robots what ingredients to use, how long to mix them, and which labels to use.
Boss: And what happens when one of the robots breaks down?
Assistant: They don't break down very often. And the robotics company will have a mechanic here within an hour.

Boss: I just can't picture it. What will we have here? A quiet building with robots rolling around doing the work?
Assistant: That's it! And these robots are great workers. They'll never come to work late and they won't call in sick. They won't take vacations. They'll work twenty-four hours a day, seven days a week, 365 days a year. And they won't go on strike.
Boss: I don't know. It sounds like a good idea, but I need time to think. What about the men and women who work here now? Most of them are good workers. They have families to support.
Assistant: Boss, that's the only problem. We won't need them anymore.

F. Comprehension questions. Listen to each question. Circle the correct answer.
1. Who wants robots in this factory?
2. How will the robots know what to do?
3. What will happen if a robot breaks down?
4. What is one problem with robots?
5. Why are robots good workers?
6. What will happen to the workers in this factory?

G. Listen and choose. Listen to each sentence. Circle the verb you hear. Several of the verbs are negatives.
1. We make ten different kinds of cough syrup.
2. One robot will measure the ingredients.
3. One robot will pour the syrup into bottles.
4. One worker will program the robots.
5. He'll type the orders into a computer.
6. Robots won't call in sick.
7. The robotics company will have a mechanic here in an hour.
8. They won't go on strike.
9. I need time to think about it.
10. We won't need the workers anymore.

H. Listen and write. Listen to each sentence. Write the verb you hear. All of the verbs are in the future tense; several are negative.
1. A second robot will mix the ingredients.
2. A fourth robot will put on the labels.
3. The last robot will pack the bottles into boxes.
4. One worker will program the robots.
5. What will we have around here?
6. They'll never come to work late.
7. They won't take vacations.
8. They'll work twenty four hours a day.
9. They won't go on strike for higher pay.
10. We won't need the workers anymore.

I. Listen and decide. You will hear a statement in the future tense. Is the grammar correct or incorrect? Circle *correct* or *incorrect.*
1. One robot will measure the ingredients.
2. A third robot pour the syrup into the bottles.
3. How these robots know what to do?
4. We'll tell them.
5. One worker will program the computer.
6. He just type the orders into a computer.
7. What will we have here?
8. They not call in sick.
9. They won't go on strike.
10. We not need the workers anymore.

7. Job Outlook

A. Fill in.
Listen to these sentences. Fill in the new vocabulary words from the list above.
1. Cashiers will be in demand in stores and supermarkets.
2. Because families are having fewer children, some teachers will lose their jobs.
3. Small farms do not make much money and many will go out of business.
4. The government publishes a book which tells about the future of many jobs.
5. This book describes job duties, working conditions, and salary.
6. Families with working mothers will have more money to spend.
7. In the future, machines will do some jobs that people do now.
8. Older cars need more repairs than newer cars.

STORY—UNIT 7—Job Outlook

Each year, the United States government publishes the *Occupational Outlook Handbook*. This large book lists over 250 kinds of jobs. It describes job duties, working conditions, education needed, and salary. Most important, it gives the job outlook. That is, it tells how many openings there will be for a job in the coming years. If the outlook is excellent, there will be a great need for workers. There will be more jobs than people. If the outlook is good, the number of jobs and the number of workers will be about the same. If the outlook is poor, there will be more workers than jobs. It will be very difficult to find work in that kind of job. This chapter will describe the job outlook for ten jobs.

The job outlook for auto mechanics is good. The number of cars will continue to grow. Because cars are so expensive, people will keep their cars longer. Their cars will need more repairs.

Computer programmers will also be in demand and the job outlook is excellent. Big and small companies will use computers for much of their work.

The outlook for cashiers in stores, supermarkets, theaters, etc. is excellent. There will be a need for more than half a million new cashiers in the next ten years.

The demand for cooks and chefs will also grow, the outlook is good in this area. The population is growing and so more people will eat out. Also, more mothers are working and families will have more money to spend.

The outlook for farmers is poor. Farms will become larger and use better machinery to plant food. Many small farms will go out of business.

The future for high school teachers is poor, also. Because families are having fewer children, schools will need fewer teachers. There will be a need for math and science teachers, but some history and English teachers will lose their jobs.

The mailmen and mailwomen who deliver the mail every day face a poor job future, too. Post offices will use more machines. And companies will send less mail. They will use computers to send information.

The job outlook for nurses is excellent for both registered nurses and licensed practical nurses. The population is increasing and people are living longer. Most jobs will open in large city hospitals and in country areas.

Painters will find good job opportunities. More jobs will open in the South and West because the population is growing in those areas. Hundreds of new houses are going up each week.

Finally, the job outlook for radio and tv technicians is excellent. Families will buy more electronic equipment, such as televisions, stereos, tape recorders, video games, etc.

The *Occupational Outlook Handbook* is in the library. It can tell you if the work you are interested in has a future or not.

F. Comprehension questions.
Listen to each question. Circle the correct answer.
1. What does the *Occupational Outlook Handbook* describe?
2. The job outlook for cooks is good. What does this mean?
3. Why is the outlook for auto mechanics good?
4. Why is the outlook for farmers poor?
5. Where will a painter have a better opportunity to find a job?
6. Which job has the best outlook for the future?

G. Listen and choose.
Listen to each sentence. Circle the verb you hear.
1. This book describes job duties.
2. This chapter will talk about ten jobs.
3. People will keep their cars longer.
4. The demand for cooks will grow.
5. More mothers are working.
6. Schools will need fewer teachers.
7. Mailmen will face a poor job future.
8. People are living longer.
9. More jobs will open in the South.
10. Families will buy more electronic equipment.

H. Listen and write.
Listen to each sentence. Write the future verb you hear.
1. There will be more jobs than people.
2. People will keep their cars longer.
3. Big and small companies will use computers.
4. Many small farms will go out of business.
5. Schools will need fewer teachers.
6. Some English teachers will lose their jobs.
7. Companies will send less mail.
8. Most jobs for nurses will open in large city hospitals.
9. Painters will find good job opportunities in the South.
10. Families will eat out more often.

I. Listen and decide.
You will hear a statement in the future tense. Is the grammar correct or incorrect? Circle *correct* or *incorrect*.
1. The number of cars continue to grow.
2. People will keep their cars longer.
3. Their cars will need more repairs.
4. The demand for cooks grow.
5. Many small farms go out of business.
6. Schools will need fewer teachers.
7. Some teachers lose their jobs.
8. Most jobs open in large city hospitals.
9. Painters will find good job opportunities.
10. Families buy more electronic equipment.

8. Drunk Driver

A. Fill in.   Listen to these sentences. Fill in the new vocabulary words from the list above.
1. All drivers on that highway pay a quarter at the toll booth.
2. Try to prevent accidents before they happen.
3. The breath test shows that Joe has a lot of liquor in his body.
4. The policeman is going to issue that driver a summons for speeding.
5. The officers are on special duty. They're looking for drunk drivers.
6. That man isn't driving in a straight line. He's weaving in and out.
7. The judge is going to suspend his license. He can't drive for two months.
8. My friend received serious injuries in the accident. She's still in the hospital.

STORY—UNIT 8—Drunk Driver

It's a holiday weekend. The police officers are sitting in a hot room receiving instructions from their captain. One of these officers is Ed Williams. He and ten other officers are on special duty. This weekend alone, over 400 people are going to die from accidents caused by drunk drivers. Over 4,000 people are going to receive serious injuries, all caused by drunk drivers. The officers are going to try to prevent these accidents before they happen.

Meanwhile, Joe Forest is enjoying himself at a family party. It's getting late and he's telling his sister that he's going to leave. She's asking him to stay and wait a few hours before he drives. "Don't worry. I'm going to be fine. I'm going to drive slowly. I only had a few drinks."

Officer Williams is at a toll booth, watching cars enter the area. A green Ford is approaching, weaving from left to right. Officer Williams stops the car and tells Joe to get out. He asks Joe to walk along the white line. He can't do it. Joe also fails the breath test. Officer Williams is telling Joe that he's going to issue him a summons. And he can't drive his car home. Joe calls his sister. She's going to come and drive him home.

This was Joe's first offense. He's going to appear in court next week. He's going to receive a $400 fine. The judge is also going to suspend his license for sixty days. This first time, other drivers were lucky. Joe didn't kill them. But what about the future, is Joe going to stop drinking and driving?

F. Comprehension questions.   Listen to each question. Circle the correct answer.
1. On a holiday weekend, when do most accidents occur?
2. How many people are going to die in accidents this weekend?
3. Why is Joe's sister worried?
4. How does Officer Williams know that Joe is probably drunk?
5. What does Officer Williams ask Joe to do?
6. What is Joe's penalty?

G. Listen and choose.   Listen to each sentence. Circle the verb you hear.
1. Over 400 people are going to die this weekend.
2. Over 4,000 people are going to receive serious injuries.
3. He's going to leave.
4. I'm going to be fine.
5. I'm going to drive slowly.
6. She's going to drive him home.
7. He's going to appear in court.
8. He's going to receive a $400 fine.
9. The judge is going to suspend his license.
10. The officers are going to try to prevent accidents.

H. Listen and write.   Listen to each sentence. Write the verb you hear.
1. Over 400 people are going to die from accidents.
2. Joe is going to drive home.
3. He's going to leave now.
4. I'm going to be fine.
5. I'm going to drive slowly.
6. Joe's sister is going to come.
7. She's going to drive him home.
8. Joe's going to appear in court.
9. The judge is going to suspend his license.
10. Is Joe going to stop?

I. Listen and decide.   You will hear a statement in the future tense. Is the grammar correct or incorrect? Circle *correct* or *incorrect*.
1. Joe is going to leave.
2. He going to drive home.
3. I'm going to be fine.
4. I going to drive slowly.
5. Officer Williams going to issue Joe a summons.
6. Joe's sister is going to come to the toll booth.
7. She's going to drive him home.
8. Joe appear in court next week.
9. The judge going to suspend his license.
10. He's going to receive a $400 fine.

9. Shoplifting

A. Fill in.   Listen to these sentences. Fill in the new vocabulary words from the list above.
1. When I don't have enough money with me, I use my credit card.
2. She'll buy a bathing suit to wear at the beach.
3. The store owner will catch her if she tries to take any clothes.
4. She'll try on many dresses before she buys one.
5. Those pants look big. Try them on in the dressing room.
6. She's going to hide a bathing suit under her clothes.
7. On the weekends, she babysits for a family with two children.
8. She'll keep the bathing suit she likes best.

STORY—UNIT 9—Shoplifting

Two teenage girls are talking together.
A: Let's go shopping for bathing suits, Berta.
B: Okay. But I'm just going to look. I don't have any money with me.
A: I don't, either. But I'm going to walk out of that store with a new bathing suit.
B: How? Are you going to use your mother's credit card?
A: No. Listen, I have an idea. We'll go into the store and look at the suits and try on lots of them. Then, we'll each keep the one we like the best. We'll just wear them out of the store under our clothes. No one will see us and we won't have to pay a penny.
B: But they give you a number when you walk into the dressing room.
A: I know. I'm going to hide one bathing suit inside another one. I'll get the number four, but I'll really have five suits.
B: Are you serious, Ann? They're going to catch you.
A: No, they aren't. Aren't you going to try it, too?
B: I don't think so. But I'll come with you. What's your mother going to say when she sees your new bathing suit?
A: I'll tell her that I got the money from babysitting.
B: You know, Ann, I don't really think that this is such a good idea.
A: So? Are you coming or not?
B: I'm coming.

F. Comprehension questions. Listen to each question. Circle the correct answer.
1. How is Ann going to pay for the bathing suit?
2. How many of the girls are going to shoplift?
3. What does Berta think of Ann's idea?
4. What is Berta going to do while Ann is shoplifting?
5. How is Ann going to hide the bathing suit when she leaves the store?
6. What's Ann going to tell her mother when she asks about the bathing suit?

G. Listen and choose. Listen to each sentence. Circle the verb you hear.
1. I'm just going to look.
2. I'm going to walk out of that store with a new bathing suit.
3. We'll look at the suits.
4. We'll each keep the one we like the best.
5. I'm going to hide one bathing suit inside another.
6. I'll really have five suits.
7. They're going to catch you.
8. Aren't you going to try it?
9. I'll come with you.
10. What's your mother going to say?

H. Listen and write. Listen to each sentence. Write the verb you hear.
1. I'm just going to look.
2. I'm going to walk out of that store with a bathing suit.
3. We'll try on lots of bathing suits.
4. We'll just wear them out under our clothes.
5. No one will see us.
6. I'm going to hide one bathing suit inside another.
7. I'll get the number four.
8. They're going to catch you.
9. What's your mother going to say?
10. I'll come with you.

I. Listen and decide. You will hear a statement in the future tense. Is the grammar correct or incorrect? Circle *correct* or *incorrect*.
1. I going to walk out of that store with a new bathing suit.
2. We'll go into the store.
3. We try on lots of bathing suits.
4. We just wear it out of the store under our clothes.
5. No one will see us.
6. I'm going to hide one bathing suit inside another.
7. They going to catch you.
8. Aren't you going to try it?
9. I come with you.
10. What your mother going to say?

10. Kangaroos

A. Fill in. Listen to these sentences. Fill in the new vocabulary words from the list above.
1. Kangaroos have small front legs and large hind legs.
2. About twenty-five kangaroos live together in that herd.
3. Kangaroos move from place to place, searching for food.
4. A marsupial is an animal which has a pouch.
5. A baby kangaroo lives in its mother's pouch.
6. A baby kangaroo grows and develops in its mother's pouch.
7. In the pouch, the baby takes hold of its mother's nipple.
8. With the nipple in its mouth, the baby nurses for many weeks.

STORY—UNIT 10—Kangaroos

Australia is the home of the kangaroo. In most parts of the world, a person must go to a zoo to see a kangaroo. In Australia, kangaroos move about in freedom in the forests and on the plains. Long ago, kangaroos were giants. They were almost ten feet tall! Today, kangaroos are about the size of a man. They are five to six feet tall and weigh about 150 pounds. Kangaroos stand on their large hind legs. They use these hind legs for jumping and, if necessary, for fighting. Close to the kangaroo's body are small front legs. These are for finding and holding food.

Kangaroos live in herds of twelve or more animals. Some herds have more than fifty kangaroos. A herd has no fixed home, it moves from place to place, searching for food. If something frightens the herd, the kangaroos jump away, all at once. Kangaroos can jump twenty-five feet or more and they can move twenty-five miles per hour.

A kangaroo is a marsupial, which means it has a pouch. A baby kangaroo lives inside its mother for only thirty to forty days. At birth, the baby is only about one inch long and it is not fully formed. Its eyes and ears are closed, it has no fur, and its hind legs are not developed. This small baby climbs up its mother's body and into her pouch. It takes hold of a nipple and stays there for many weeks, nursing and developing. Soon, its eyes open and its ears form. It grows fur. Finally, the baby kangaroo lets go of the nipple and looks outside. Soon, it climbs in and out of the pouch easily. At six months of age, the young kangaroo leaves the pouch. Now it's called a joey.

F. Comprehension questions. Listen to each question. Circle the correct answer.
1. What does a herd of kangaroos do when it's frightened?
2. Why doesn't a herd have a fixed home?
3. What do kangaroos use their hind legs for?
4. How does the baby kangaroo look at birth?
5. How does the small baby get into its mother's pouch?
6. At what age can a baby kangaroo live outside its mother's pouch?

G. Listen and choose. Listen to each sentence. Circle the verb you hear.
1. Kangaroos move about in freedom.
2. Kangaroos weigh about 150 pounds.
3. They stand on large hind legs.
4. A herd has no fixed home.
5. A herd moves from place to place.
6. Some herds have more than fifty kangaroos.
7. A baby kangaroo lives inside its mother for thirty to forty days.
8. This small baby climbs into its mother's pouch.
9. It grows fur.
10. Kangaroos live in Australia.

H. Listen and write. Listen to each sentence. Write the verb you hear.
1. Kangaroos move about in freedom.
2. They live in Australia.
3. Kangaroos stand on their large hind legs.
4. A herd moves from place to place.
5. The kangaroos jump away, all at once.
6. A marsupial has a pouch.
7. The baby kangaroo lives in its mother's pouch for many weeks.
8. It takes hold of a nipple.
9. Its eyes open.
10. It climbs in and out of the pouch easily.

I. Listen and decide. You will hear a statement in the present tense. Is the grammar correct or incorrect? Circle *correct* or *incorrect*.
1. A kangaroo weigh about 150 pounds.
2. Kangaroos stand on their large hind legs.
3. They use these hind legs for jumping.
4. A herd have no fixed home.
5. A baby kangaroo live inside its mother for thirty to forty days.
6. The kangaroos jump away, all at once.
7. The baby climb into its mother's pouch.
8. It stay there for many weeks.
9. It grow fur.
10. Kangaroos move about in freedom in Australia.

11. Toy World

A. Fill in. Listen to these sentences. Fill in the new vocabulary words from the list above.
1. I work the second shift at the factory, from 3:00 to 11:00.
2. Ford Motor Company manufactures cars.

3. It's cold today. The temperature is 20 .
4. When work is slow at our company, many workers get laid off.
5. This factory receives radio parts from different companies. The workers here assemble the radios.
6. This part is too big. It doesn't fit into the hole.
7. Two men take the boxes and load them onto a truck.
8. Each worker on an assembly line does a different job.

STORY—UNIT 11—Toy World

It's July. The temperature is 89°. The workers at Toy World are busy, getting ready for Christmas. Toy World manufactures children's toys. It operates many short assembly lines. This area assembles dolls. The doll parts arrive from Hong Kong. They come in large boxes, one for arms, another for legs, one for bodies, another for heads. Bill and James unpack the boxes and put the parts on the line. They put a head, a body, one left arm, one right arm, one left leg, and one right leg in each box. Olga installs a voice box in the back of each doll. The dolls can say "Mommy," "Daddy," and "night-night." Then, Tony and Marta assemble the dolls. Sometimes a part doesn't fit, so there are extra parts next to the line. Then Ana dresses the dolls. She puts pink pajamas on some dolls, yellow pajamas on others. George packs the dolls in boxes. The front of each box is clear plastic so that children and their parents can see the doll in the box. He puts the smaller boxes into a larger one. Mark loads these boxes onto a truck.

Toy World is busy from May to November. During these months, it operates three shifts. But all the toys have to be on store shelves by November. From December to April, business is slow and many workers get laid off. Usually, only one shift operates.

F. Comprehension questions. Listen to each question. Circle the correct answer.
1. What does Toy World manufacture?
2. What does Ana put on the dolls?
3. What can't the dolls say?
4. When do the toys have to be on the store shelves?
5. What happens to many workers in December?
6. How many shifts operate in June?

G. Listen and choose. Listen to each sentence. Circle the verb you hear.
1. Toy World manufactures children's toys.
2. This area assembles dolls.
3. The parts arrive from Hong Kong.
4. Bill and James unpack the boxes.
5. Olga installs a voice box.
6. Tony and Marta assemble the dolls.
7. They have extra parts next to the line.
8. George puts the dolls in boxes.
9. It operates three shifts.
10. Many workers get laid off.

H. Listen and write. Listen to each sentence. Write the verb you hear.
1. It operates many short assembly lines.
2. The parts come in large boxes.
3. Bill and James put the parts on the line.
4. Sometimes a part doesn't fit.
5. Then Ana dresses the dolls.
6. She puts pink pajamas on some dolls.

7. George packs the dolls in boxes.
8. Mark loads these boxes onto a truck.
9. Only one shift operates.
10. Many workers get laid off.

I. Listen and decide. You will hear a statement in the present tense. Is the grammar correct or incorrect? Circle *correct* or *incorrect*.
1. Toy World manufactures children's toys.
2. It operate many short assembly lines.
3. This area assemble dolls.
4. Bill and James unpack the boxes.
5. Olga install a voice box.
6. Sometimes a part don't fit.
7. She puts pink pajamas on some dolls.
8. George packs the dolls in boxes.
9. Mark load these boxes onto a truck.
10. Many workers get laid off.

12. Adult Day Care

A. Fill in. Listen to these sentences. Fill in the new vocabulary words from the list above.
1. John needed physical therapy to help him walk again after his accident.
2. My father is recovering quickly after his accident. He'll be home from the hospital next week.
3. Many families are participating in this program.
4. After he lost his arm in the accident, he received an artificial one.
5. My mother is becoming forgetful. She can't remember people's names.
6. The woman who lives above us is elderly. She's over ninety years old.
7. After his stroke, John couldn't move the left side of his body.
8. After his operation, he was a patient in the hospital for two weeks.

STORY—UNIT 12—Adult Day Care

David Brown and Ann Ramos are two patients participating in the Adult Day Care program at Mercy Hospital.

David Brown is seventy-two years old. He's friendly and likes to talk. He lives with his wife in a small apartment in the city. But David is becoming forgetful. His wife says, "He'll heat up some soup, then forget to turn off the stove." She is sixty-one and still works. She's worried about leaving her husband alone by himself.

Ann Ramos is eighty and lives with her daughter, who is sixty. Her daughter says that she needs a break. "Mom follows me everywhere. She follows me from room to room when I clean. She sits down next to me when I read the newspaper. She even follows me out of the house when I take out the garbage. I need a break and she does, too."

And so, several times a week, David and Ann's families take them to the Adult Day Care Center. Many hospitals now offer this program. Patients come to the center for a full or half day, from one

to five days a week. All the patients live with their families and most are elderly. Some are becoming forgetful, others are recovering from an operation, a stroke, or an accident.

The Center offers many activities. Patients learn crafts, such as sewing, woodworking, and painting. Many patients like to cook and they bake fresh bread or other snacks daily. Several men and women enjoy playing checkers, bingo, cards, or other games. All the patients enjoy talking, singing, and being with one another.

Some patients also need physical therapy. At Mercy Hospital, one man is learning to walk with an artificial leg. One woman had a stroke and cannot move her right arm. She is doing simple exercises and the movement is slowly returning.

Mrs. Carol Johnson is the director of the Center. She states, "We are offering both the patients and their families a valuable service. Patients have the opportunity to get out of their homes. Husbands, wives, or grown children can work or have a break. Most important, families are able to stay together."

F. Comprehension questions. Listen to each question. Circle the correct answer.
1. Why does Mrs. Brown send her husband to the Adult Day Care Center?
2. Why is Ann Ramos's daughter sending her to the Adult Day Care Center?
3. Where do the patients in this program live?
4. What is one activity that all the patients enjoy?
5. Why do some patients need physical therapy?
6. How does the Adult Day Care Center help families stay together?

G. Listen and choose. Listen to each sentence. Circle the verb you hear.
1. They are participating in the Adult Day Care program.
2. David lives in a small apartment in the city.
3. He's becoming forgetful.
4. His wife still works.
5. Mom follows me everywhere.
6. Patients come to the Center for a full or half day.
7. The Center offers many services.
8. Some patients bake fresh bread.
9. One man is learning to walk.
10. We are offering the patients and their families a valuable service.

H. Listen and write. Listen to each sentence. Write the verb you hear. Some verbs are present tense, some are present continuous.
1. David is becoming forgetful.
2. Ann lives with her daughter.
3. Ann's daughter needs a break.
4. Their families take them to the Adult Day Care Center.
5. All the patients live with their families.
6. Some are recovering from accidents.
7. Patients learn crafts.
8. Some patients need physical therapy.
9. One woman is doing simple exercises.
10. The movement in her right arm is returning.

I. Listen and decide. You will hear a statement. Is the grammar correct or incorrect? Circle *correct* or *incorrect*.
1. David and Ann participating in the Adult Day Care program.
2. David live with his wife.

3. David is become forgetful.
4. Mom follow me everywhere.
5. Many hospitals offer this program.
6. All the patients live with their families.
7. Some becoming forgetful.
8. The Center offer many services.
9. Some patients need physical therapy.
10. One man is learn to walk.

13. Problems at School

A. Fill in.   Listen to these sentences. Fill in the new vocabulary words from the list above.
1. He was away for three days on a business trip.
2. When a student fools around in class, the teacher seats the student alone in a corner.
3. No, he isn't divorced. He's a widower.
4. Please pay attention when I give the directions.
5. If this behavior continues, the teacher is going to call her parents.
6. I agree with you. He's an excellent student.
7. She lives in a quiet neighborhood.
8. When a student doesn't do his or her homework, the teacher sends a note to the student's parents.

STORY—UNIT 13—Problems at School

Teacher: Mr. Toma? I'm glad to meet you. I'm Miss Hanson, Mario's teacher.

Parent: Thank you for sending me this note. I'm sorry to hear Mario is being a problem.

T: I'm not sure what's happening to Mario. He's usually an excellent student. He completes all his work and he's quiet in class. Then, last month, he just changed.

P: How?

T: Well, he fools around in class. And he doesn't pay attention. He talks to the children who sit near him when he should be reading or writing.

P: Mario? I'm surprised. What about his work?

T: He doesn't do it. When I ask the class to do an exercise, he sits and looks out the window. Sometimes he draws pictures on his papers. And he doesn't bring in any homework.

P: I don't know what to say. I don't understand what's happening to him.

T: Is anything different at home?

P: Well, yes. You know that I'm a widower and Mario is my only child. I have a new job and I need to take a lot of business trips. While I'm away, I leave Mario at his grandmother's.

T: How much are you away?

P: Oh, three or four days each week, sometimes five.

T: Does Mario like staying at his grandmother's?

P: Not too much. She's old and worries about him. She lives in an apartment building, so he doesn't go out and play after school. He doesn't have any friends in her neighborhood.

T: Do you have any brothers or sisters?

P: Yes, my sister lives a few blocks from me. Mario wants to stay with her. She loves children, but she has three of her own. Now I'm not sure what to do.

T: Why don't you talk with your mother and your sister? Then talk with Mario. Mario is telling us that he's unhappy.

P: I agree. Thank you for talking with me. And I'm very sorry about my son's behavior. I'll give you a call next week.

T: Thank you, Mr. Toma.

P: Thank you, Miss Hanson.

F. Comprehension questions.   Listen to each question. Circle the correct answer.
1. Why did Mr. Toma come to see Mario's teacher?
2. What does Mario do when the teacher gives an assignment?
3. Who takes care of Mario when his father is away?
4. What is probably the reason for Mario's behavior?
5. Who does Mario want to stay with?
6. What do you think Mr. Toma should do?

G. Listen and choose.   Listen to each sentence. Circle the verb you hear. Several of the verbs are negatives.
1. He fools around in class.
2. He doesn't pay attention.
3. He talks to the other children.
4. He doesn't do his work.
5. He looks out the window.
6. He doesn't bring in his homework.
7. I don't know what to say.
8. I don't understand him.
9. I take a lot of business trips.
10. He doesn't have any friends in her neighborhood.

H. Listen and write.   Listen to each sentence. Write the verb you hear. Several of the verbs are negatives.
1. He fools around in class.
2. He doesn't pay attention.
3. He doesn't do his work.
4. He draws pictures on his papers.
5. I don't understand him.
6. I leave Mario at his grandmother's.
7. He doesn't play outside after school.
8. She lives in an apartment.
9. My sister loves children.
10. I agree.

I. Listen and decide.   You will hear a negative statement. Is the grammar correct or incorrect? Circle *correct* or *incorrect*.
1. He not pay attention.
2. He doesn't pay attention.
3. He don't do his work.
4. He doesn't bring in his homework.
5. I no understand.
6. I don't know.
7. He doesn't go out after school.
8. He no play after school.
9. He no have any friends in her neighborhood.
10. Mario doesn't like staying with his grandmother.

14. A Professional

A. Fill in.   Listen to these sentences. Fill in the new vocabulary words from the list above.
1. The thief stole their tv and their stereo.
2. Business men and women carry their papers in a briefcase.
3. She put together the bicycle with a screwdriver.
4. I usually take about $100 in cash with me when I go to the store.
5. Don't touch the money in my desk. I'm saving it to buy a ring.
6. On a typical day, I get up at 7:00.
7. Please put the plates and silverware on the table. It's time to eat.
8. The boy climbed up the tree to get into the window on the second floor.

STORY—UNIT 14—A Professional

Richard Williams works hard. He's intelligent, careful, and fast. His work is dangerous. Richard thinks of himself as a professional— a professional thief.

Yesterday was a typical day. Richard dressed in a business suit, took his briefcase, and drove to a town about ten miles from his home. He parked his car in a busy area, then began to walk along the street. No one looked at him. He was another businessman, walking to work.

At 8:05, Richard saw what he wanted. A man was leaving his house. Richard walked around the block again. At 8:10, he watched a woman leave the same house. After she left, Richard worked quickly. He walked to the side of the house and stood behind a tree. He took a screwdriver out of his briefcase and quickly opened the window and climbed in. First, he looked through the desk in the living room. He found $200 in cash. In the dining room, he put the silverware into his briefcase. The next stop was the bedroom. Richard stole a diamond ring and an emerald necklace. Richard passed a color tv, a stereo, and a camera, but he didn't touch them. Everything had to fit into his briefcase. In less than five minutes, Richard climbed back out the window. He looked around carefully, then began his walk down the street again. No one looked at him. He was just another businessman, walking to work.

F. Comprehension questions.   Listen to each question. Circle the correct answer.
1. Why did Richard wear a business suit?
2. What did Richard do after the man left his house?
3. Why didn't anyone see Richard get into the house?
4. Why didn't Richard take the television set?
5. How long did Richard stay in the house?
6. What did Richard steal?

G. Listen and choose.   Listen to each sentence. Circle the verb you hear.
1. Richard thinks of himself as a professional.
2. Yesterday was a typical day.
3. Richard always takes his briefcase with him.
4. Richard drove to a town about ten miles from his home.
5. He began to walk along the street.
6. At 8:05, Richard saw what he wanted.
7. He stood behind a tree.
8. He stole a diamond ring.
9. Everything had to fit in his briefcase.
10. Richard works hard.

H. Listen and write.   Listen to each sentence. Write the verb you hear.
1. Richard drove to a town about ten miles from his home.
2. Richard saw a man leave his house.
3. Ten minutes later, a woman left the same house.
4. Richard stood behind a tree.
5. He took a screwdriver out of his briefcase.
6. He found $200 in cash.
7. He put the silverware in his briefcase.
8. The next stop was the bedroom.
9. Richard stole a diamond ring.
10. He began his walk down the street again.

I. Listen and decide.   You will hear a statement in the past tense. Is the grammar correct or incorrect? Circle *correct* or *incorrect*.
1. Yesterday is a typical day.
2. Richard drive to a town about ten miles from his home.
3. He began to walk along the street.
4. Richard saw a man leaving his house.
5. A woman leave the same house.
6. Richard stand behind a tree.
7. He took a screwdriver out of his briefcase.
8. He find $200 in cash.
9. The next stop is the bedroom.
10. Everything had to fit in his briefcase.

15. Marco Polo

A. Fill in.   Listen to these sentences. Fill in the new vocabulary words from the list above.
1. Marco Polo dictated his story to a friend. His friend wrote down what he said.
2. In his descriptions, Marco Polo gave the people a picture of what he saw.
3. In the public baths, people washed many times a week.
4. Trees are covered by bark.
5. The people dug into the earth and found black stones.
6. Marco Polo's stories amazed people. They were surprised to read about a country that was so different.
7. Kublai Khan was the powerful emperor of China in 1275.
8. The highways, medicine, and postal system of China were more advanced than those of Europe.

STORY—UNIT 15—Marco Polo

One of the most famous travelers in all of history was Marco Polo. At the age of seventeen, he left Italy with his father and uncle. It took them more than three years to cross the mountains and deserts of Asia. In the year 1275, they reached the palace of Kublai Khan, the great emperor of China. They stayed in China for almost twenty years, as guests of the emperor. He sent them on many trips around his empire. They were amazed at what they saw. China was a country far more advanced than Italy or any other country in Europe.

After he returned to Italy, Marco Polo dictated many of his stories to a friend. His book, *Description of the World*, became the most popular book in Europe. People found it difficult to believe his stories of people, animals, places, and things. They were so different from Europe at that time. These are a few of Marco Polo's descriptions.

In one area of China, there were black stones. People dug them out of the mountains. They lit the black stones and they burned very slowly, giving off heat. The people used these stones to cook and to heat their homes.

In China there was a great system of highways. These highways had two lanes paved with stone or brick. Men planted trees every ten feet to keep the sun off of travelers' heads.

The Chinese people were also very clean. In every town, there were many public baths. Everyone bathed at least three times a week. Rich families built baths in their homes and bathed daily.

China was one of the first countries to use paper money. The government made bills from the bark of a special tree. They signed the money and stamped it with the royal seal. The people could use this money the same as they could use gold or silver.

On one of his trips in the south of China, Marco saw a strange animal which lived along the rivers. It looked like a large piece of wood and was more than ten feet long. In the front, it had two small legs. Its eyes were very large. Its mouth was big enough to eat a man and its teeth were long and sharp.

Most people believed Marco Polo's stories. But others told him that they did not believe his descriptions. He answered that he did not tell half of what he saw.

F. Comprehension questions. Listen to each question. Circle the correct answer.
1. How did Marco Polo travel to China?
2. How many years did Marco Polo stay in China?
3. How did people in Europe heat their houses in 1275?
4. Why were Europeans amazed that China had paved highways?
5. What animal did Marco Polo see in the south of China?
6. Did everyone believe Marco Polo's stories?

G. Listen and choose. Listen to each sentence. Write the regular past verb that you hear.
1. In the year 1275, they reached the palace of Kublai Khan.
2. They stayed in China for almost twenty years.
3. Marco Polo dictated many of his stories to a friend.
4. These black stones burned very slowly.
5. The people used these stones to cook.
6. Men planted trees every ten feet.
7. Everyone bathed at least three times a week.
8. The government officials signed the money.
9. They stamped it with the royal seal.
10. The strange animal looked like a large piece of wood.

H. Listen and write. Listen to each sentence. Write the irregular past verb that you hear.
1. Marco Polo left Italy with his father and uncle.
2. It took them more than three years to reach China.
3. The emperor sent them on many trips around his empire.
4. Marco Polo's book became the most popular book in Europe.
5. People dug black stones out of the mountains.
6. They lit them.
7. The highways had two lanes.
8. Rich families built baths in their homes.
9. The government made bills from the bark of a special tree.
10. Marco saw a strange animal in the south of China.

I. Listen and decide. You will hear a statement in the past tense. Is the grammar correct or incorrect? Circle *correct* or *incorrect*.
1. Marco Polo leave Italy with his father and uncle.
2. They reached the palace of Kublai Khan in 1275.
3. They stay in China for almost twenty years.
4. Marco Polo dictate many of his stories to a friend.
5. People dug black stones out of the mountains.
6. They burn very slowly.
7. The highways have two lanes.
8. Rich families built baths in their homes.
9. The government make bills from bark.
10. They signed the bills.

16. Space Shuttle

A. Fill in. Listen to these sentences. Fill in the new vocabulary words from the list above.
1. A space shuttle can be used over and over again.
2. Three to five astronauts fly on each space shuttle.
3. The rocket lifted the space ship into the sky.
4. John Young, a top pilot, sat at the controls of Columbia.
5. The space shuttle can launch satellites through the large cargo doors.
6. Satellites circle the earth. Some send radio and tv programs from one country to another.
7. The parachute opened and took the rocket safely down into the ocean.
8. Columbia circled the earth in an orbit 170 miles high.

STORY—UNIT 16—Space Shuttle

A shuttle is a vehicle that travels back and forth frequently. A space shuttle is a vehicle that travels into space and then back again. It can be used again and again.

On April 12, 1981, the United States launched the first space shuttle, Columbia. The morning of April 12 was clear and sunny. Two astronauts, John Young and Robert Crippen, sat at the controls. At 7:00, they fired the engines. The booster rockets and the space shuttle lifted off into the air. Two minutes later, 28 miles up, the booster rockets and the space shuttle separated. Parachutes took the rockets safely down into the Atlantic Ocean where ships waited to pick them up. Columbia continued to climb to an orbit of 170 miles above earth. The space shuttle circled the earth thirty-six times. During this time, Young and Crippen tested the equipment on the shuttle. They also opened and closed the large cargo doors. Two days later, on April 14, Young fired the shuttle's engines. This slowed down the spacecraft. Young, a top pilot, took the controls of Columbia. He entered the earth's atmosphere and headed toward California. At 1:21 p.m., Young made a perfect landing at Edwards Air Force Base.

Since this first launch, Columbia has traveled into space more than seven times. The second shuttle, Challenger, is also operating.

And the United States is building two more space shuttles. It is planning over sixty more shuttle flights. Some will launch satellites through the cargo doors. Some will try to manufacture drugs and chemicals in space. One will carry a large telescope into orbit which will send pictures back to earth. It is possible that some day in the future, space shuttles will carry passengers to the moon.

F. Comprehension questions.   Listen to each question. Circle the correct answer.
1. How many times can a shuttle be used?
2. What happened to the booster rockets?
3. How many times did Columbia circle the earth?
4. How did Young slow down the spacecraft?
5. How many space shuttles will the United States have?
6. Why are the cargo doors important?

G. Listen and choose.   Listen to each sentence. Circle the verb you hear.
1. A shuttle travels back and forth frequently.
2. The United States launched the first space shuttle, Columbia.
3. Two astronauts sat at the controls.
4. The astronauts fired the engines.
5. The booster rockets and the space shuttle separated.
6. The space shuttle circled the earth thirty-six times.
7. They tested the equipment on the shuttle.
8. Young entered the earth's atmosphere.
9. Some shuttles will launch satellites.
10. One will carry a large telescope into orbit.

H. Listen and write.   Listen to each sentence. Write the verb you hear.
1. The United States launched the first space shuttle.
2. The space shuttle lifted off into the air.
3. The booster rockets and the space shuttle separated.
4. Ships waited to pick the rockets up.
5. Columbia continued to climb to an orbit of 170 miles above earth.
6. Young and Crippen tested the equipment on the space ship.
7. They opened and closed the cargo doors.
8. Young fired the shuttle's engines.
9. He entered the earth's atmosphere.
10. He headed toward California.

I. Listen and decide.   You will hear a statement in the past time. Is the grammar correct or incorrect? Circle *correct* or *incorrect*.
1. The United States launched the first space shuttle.
2. They fire the engines.
3. The booster rockets and the space shuttle separate.
4. Columbia continued to climb to an orbit of 170 miles above earth.
5. It circle the earth thirty-six times.
6. They also open and close the cargo doors.
7. Young fired the shuttle's engines.
8. This slow down the spacecraft.
9. Young enter the earth's atmosphere.
10. He headed toward California.

17. Lottery Winners

A. Fill in.   Listen to these sentences. Fill in the new vocabulary words from the list above.
1. I didn't study for the test. If I don't do well, it's my own fault.
2. My father isn't working now and he doesn't know what to do with his time. He's bored.
3. In the summer, I like to spend my time working in the garden.
4. I dream of winning a million dollars.
5. As soon as she received her paycheck, she spent the money for new clothes.
6. Money in the bank brings security. You know that if you need it, it's there.
7. After he won the lottery, he quit his job.
8. She never had the opportunity to go to college because she didn't have the time or the money.

STORY—UNIT 17—Lottery Winners

Did you ever dream of winning the lottery? So have millions of other people. Every day, millions of Americans buy lottery tickets. They are hoping to win $50,000, $100,000, one million dollars or more. What happens after a person wins the lottery?

When a person wins a million dollars, he or she doesn't receive a check for the total amount. The person receives $50,000 a year for twenty years. Also, he or she must pay taxes. After taxes, a million-dollar winner receives from $25,000 to $40,000 a year for twenty years. This is a lot of extra spending money.

What have some people done with their money? Let's look at four past winners.

Lisa K. wanted to be an artist, but she didn't have enough money to go to school. She was working at a job she didn't enjoy. In August, Lisa bought one ticket and won, two million dollars. She quit her job three weeks later and is now attending art school. Lisa says, "If I don't become an artist, it's my own fault. I have the opportunity now."

Mark L. was a car salesman. He worked seven days a week and had little time for family life. After he won the lottery, he quit working. Now he spends his time bowling, working in the garden, and fixing things in his house. But, he's bored. He doesn't want to sell cars again, but he isn't sure what he wants to do with his life.

Mabel S. was over sixty when she won a million dollars. She started to spend her money immediately. She bought a new car, new clothes, and new furniture for her house. She paid for her son's college tuition and bought a car for him, too. Then she gave all her grandchildren money. After a few months, she had no money left to pay her bills. Also, she forgot about her taxes and didn't have enough money to pay them. She plans to spend her money more carefully next year.

Jack B. is one of the small number of winners who did not quit his job. Jack still teaches at a nearby school. But he and his wife now have a new car in the garage. They take their four children on an interesting vacation every year. And they don't worry about sending their children to college. They say that money brings security and gives a person opportunities, but it doesn't bring happiness.

F. Comprehension questions.   Listen to each question. Circle the correct answer.
1. How many people buy lottery tickets every day?
2. After taxes, how much money does a million-dollar winner receive each year?

3. Mark was a car salesman. What is he doing now?
4. What did most of the winners do after they won the lottery?
5. What is Mabel going to do with her money next year?
6. According to Jack and his wife, what does money bring a person?

G. Listen and choose.   Listen to each sentence. Circle the verb you hear. All the verbs are in the negative.
1. A winner doesn't receive a check for the total amount.
2. Lisa didn't have enough money to go to school.
3. She was working at a job she didn't enjoy.
4. If I don't become an artist, it's my own fault.
5. Mark doesn't want to sell cars again.
6. He doesn't know what to do with his time.
7. Mabel didn't have enough money to pay her taxes.
8. Jack didn't quit his job.
9. They don't worry about sending their children to college.
10. Money doesn't bring happiness.

H. Listen and write.   Listen to each sentence. Write the verb you hear. All the verbs are in the negative.
1. Jack didn't quit his job.
2. He doesn't worry about sending his children to college.
3. Lisa didn't enjoy her job.
4. If she doesn't become an artist, it's her own fault.
5. She didn't have the opportunity to go to school before this.
6. Mark doesn't know what to do with his time.
7. He didn't have time for his family.
8. He doesn't want to sell insurance again.
9. Mabel didn't spend her money carefully.
10. She didn't have enough money to pay her taxes.

I. Listen and decide.   You will hear a statement. Is the grammar correct or incorrect? Circle *correct* or *incorrect*. Listen for *don't, doesn't,* and *didn't.*
1. A million-dollar winner no receive a check for the total amount.
2. Lisa didn't have enough money to go to college.
3. If I not become an artist, it's my own fault.
4. Lisa not enjoy her job.
5. Mark doesn't want to sell cars again.
6. He not know what he wants to do.
7. Mabel no have enough money to pay her taxes.
8. Jack not quit his job.
9. They don't worry about sending their children to college.
10. Money doesn't bring happiness.

18. Unemployment

A. Fill in.   Listen to these sentences. Fill in the new vocabulary words from the list above.
1. Al lost his job. He's filing a claim for unemployment.
2. Bob got laid off. As a matter of fact, all fifty workers at his plant got laid off.
3. He's having no luck finding a new job.

4. People aren't buying as many big cars. One of the big car plants closed down.
5. Some months Al sold eight or nine cars, other months he sold eleven or twelve. He averaged about ten cars a month.
6. Very few people are buying cars. The boss let three car salesmen go.
7. The interest rates are 14 percent.
8. The management decided to move the plant from this country to Singapore.

STORY—UNIT 18—Unemployment

Al: Is this the right line to file a claim?

Bob: Yeah. It's the same line for everything. You just stand here and wait.

Al: Oh. Is there always such a long line?

Bob: Every week. Sometimes longer. Is this your first time here?

Al: Yes.

Bob: What happened? Your plant close down?

Al: No. I'm a car salesman, or, I was a car salesman. But we just aren't selling cars. It's the interest rates. Two years ago, I averaged ten new cars a month. Do you know how many cars I sold last month? One. One car to a lady who had the cash. But the interest rates are up again. The boss let three of us go. How about you?

Bob: I worked at a vacuum cleaner plant with about fifty workers. We put in a good day's work. But the machinery was getting old. As a matter of fact, the whole plant was old. So the management decided to build a new plant. You know where? In Singapore. The workers here made about seven dollars an hour, a couple of people made eight or nine an hour. You know how much they're paying the workers in Singapore? $2.50 an hour. Who can live on $2.50 an hour? Anyway, all fifty of us got laid off.

Al: How long ago was that?

Bob: They closed down ten months ago.

Al: Any luck finding another job?

Bob: Nothing. I have one, sometimes two, interviews a week. Last week I thought I had something. They liked my experience with machines. But I never heard from them again.

Al: At least you know something about machines. All I can do is talk.

Bob: Maybe you'll talk yourself into another job. Good luck. I'll see you here next week.

Al: I hope not. I hope I'll have something by then.

F. Comprehension questions.   Listen to each question. Circle the correct answer.
1. Why is Al standing in line?
2. According to Al, why aren't people buying cars as they used to?
3. Why did the management decide to move to Singapore?
4. How much money did most of the people in the vacuum cleaner plant make?
5. Is Bob really looking for another job?
6. How long does Al think he will collect unemployment?

G. Listen and choose.   Listen to each sentence. Circle the verb you hear.
1. You just wait.
2. I sold cars.
3. I averaged ten cars a month.

4. I worked at a vacuum cleaner plant.
5. The management decided to open a new plant.
6. The workers here made about seven dollars an hour.
7. They closed down about seven months ago.
8. I have one interview a week.
9. They liked my experience with machines.
10. You know something about machines.

H.   Listen and write.   Listen to each sentence. Write the verb you hear.
1. What happened?
2. I was a car salesman.
3. I averaged ten new cars a month.
4. Last month I only sold one car.
5. I worked at a vacuum cleaner plant.
6. We put in a good day's work.
7. A couple of people made eight or nine dollars an hour.
8. All fifty of us got laid off.
9. They closed down ten months ago.
10. I never heard from them again.

I.   Listen and decide.   You will hear a statement in the past tense. Is the grammar correct or incorrect? Circle *correct* or *incorrect*.
1. What happen?
2. I average about ten new cars a month.
3. I sold one car last month.
4. The lady have the cash.
5. The management decided to build a new plant.
6. All fifty of us get laid off.
7. They closed down ten months ago.
8. Last week, I thought I had something.
9. They like my experience with machines.
10. I never heard from them again.

19. Mount St. Helens

A.   Fill in.   Listen to these sentences. Fill in the new vocabulary words from the list above.
1. The climber placed a flag at the summit of the mountain.
2. The slopes of the mountain are covered with snow.
3. Vesuvius was a volcano that erupted in the year 79 A.D.
4. Tremors shook the earth and the trees.
5. Only a few people survived the explosion; most died.
6. After the fire, the trees were only hot ash.
7. The eruption sent rocks and trees into the air.
8. Yellowstone Park is a recreation area with hiking, camping, swimming, and many other activities.

STORY—UNIT 19—Mount St. Helens

Most volcanoes are quiet. They rest peacefully for hundreds of years. No one pays much attention to them.

Mount St. Helens was one of these volcanoes. It's located in the United States in southwest Washington and it covers over 35 square miles. Until 1980, it was a beautiful recreation area. Fishermen caught large fish in its lakes and rivers, families camped on its slopes, and men and women climbed to its summit. Its last eruption had been 123 years ago. No one was worried about another one.

Then, in March 1980, Mount St. Helens began to make noises. At first, there were tremors. Then, small eruptions occurred. Some residents left immediately. Others felt there was no danger. Nothing was going to happen.

But on the morning of May 18, 1980, the mountain blew its top. With the power of twenty-five atomic bombs, Mount St. Helens exploded. Clouds of dust and ash rose more than twelve miles into the sky. Rocks and mud crashed down the slopes.

Unfortunately, many people were still living, camping, or working in the area. Over forty people lost their lives. Others were rescued.

Robert Barker was fishing with his family when the explosion occurred. He reported that the morning of May 18 was strange. No birds were singing. The air was still. Then, he saw that a large black cloud was coming toward them. In minutes, day turned into night. He called his family to their van and they started on the slow dark ride away from the mountain. All the time, hot ash was raining on them.

But other people were not so lucky.

David Johnston, a volcano expert, was standing near the summit of the mountain. At 8:31 a.m. he radioed, "This is it!" He was never heard from again.

Six friends were camping on the slopes of Mount St. Helens. They were cooking breakfast when they heard the explosion and the hot ash began to fall on them. Four of them survived. The bodies of the other two were found a week later.

Mount St. Helens is peaceful now. But its slopes are empty. It will be many years before fish, animals, plants, and trees will again live on the mountain.

F.   Comprehension questions.   Listen to each question. Circle the correct answer.
1. How often do most volcanoes erupt?
2. When was the last time Mount St. Helens erupted?
3. What time of day did the explosion occur?
4. What was the area like immediately before the explosion?
5. What was David Johnston doing when the explosion occurred?
6. What does Mount St. Helens look like now?

G.   Listen and choose.   Listen to each sentence. Circle the verb you hear.
1. Many people were living on the mountain.
2. Many people were camping in the area.
3. Robert Barker was fishing with his family.
4. Nothing was going to happen.
5. No birds were singing.
6. A large black cloud was moving toward them.
7. Hot ash was raining on them.
8. David Johnston was standing near the summit of the mountain.
9. Six friends were camping on the slopes of the mountain.
10. They were cooking breakfast.

H.   Listen and write.   Listen to each sentence. Write the verb you hear.
1. Nothing was going to happen.
2. Many people were working in the area.
3. Many people were camping in the area.
4. Robert Barker was fishing with his family.

5. No birds were singing.
6. A large black cloud was coming toward them.
7. Hot ash was raining on their van.
8. David Johnston was standing near the summit of the mountain.
9. Six friends were camping on the slopes.
10. They were cooking breakfast.

I. Listen and decide. You will hear a statement in the past continuous tense. Is the grammar correct or incorrect? Circle *correct* or *incorrect*.

1. Many people fishing.
2. Many people were camping.
3. Other people was working.
4. Nothing going to happen.
5. Robert Barker was fishing.
6. A large black cloud was coming toward them.
7. Hot ash was rain on them.
8. David Johnston standing near the summit.
9. Six friends camping.
10. They were cook breakfast.

20. The Titanic

A. Fill in. Listen to these sentences. Fill in the new vocabulary words from the list above.

1. An iceberg is a small or large mountain of ice in the water.
2. After it hit an iceberg, the Titanic sank to the bottom of the ocean.
3. Every ship carries lifeboats in case of an accident at sea.
4. The iceberg ripped a large hole in the side of the ship.
5. The icebergs were only a few miles ahead. The ship was approaching them at full speed.
6. The passengers were in high spirits as their trip began.
7. The luxury ship had a swimming pool, three dining rooms, bars, libraries, and game rooms.
8. As the Titanic sank, people prayed, talked, or held one another. There was no panic.

STORY—UNIT 20—The Titanic

Millionaire Arthur Ryerson stepped on board the Titanic in high spirits. He was going to enjoy this trip across the Atlantic. This was the Titanic's first voyage, a trip from England to New York City. Her decks filled with libraries, smoking rooms, dining rooms, a gymnasium, and a swimming pool promised a relaxing week.

When the Titanic pulled out of port on April 10, 1912, she was carrying 2,224 passengers and crew. The first four days of the trip were clear, calm, and cold. Arthur Ryerson spent his days talking, walking, and playing cards with several of his friends. All the passengers were enjoying their days aboard the luxury ship. None of them knew of the danger ahead. They were approaching icebergs.

The evening of April 14 was relaxed and friendly. By 11:30, most passengers were sleeping or getting ready for bed. Other passengers were reading, drinking, or writing letters. The band was finishing for the evening. Arthur Ryerson was playing cards with three of his friends.

Out in the cold, one of the crewmen was standing watch. Suddenly, up ahead, he saw something in the water. He immediately rang three bells and radioed the engine room, "Iceberg, right ahead! Stop!" It was too late. The iceberg ripped a 300-foot hole in the Titanic's right side. The ship was filling with water and sinking fast.

There was no panic on board. Arthur Ryerson was one of the men who helped women and children into the lifeboats. When he saw there would be no room for himself or any of the other men on the ship, Ryerson and his three friends returned to the smoking room and their game of cards. They were still playing as the Titanic sank into the icy waters. On that cold evening in 1912, 1,513 people lost their lives in one of the worst sea disasters in history.

F. Comprehension questions. Listen to each question. Circle the correct answer.

1. Where was the ship traveling?
2. Where did the ship hit the iceberg?
3. What was Arthur Ryerson doing when the Titanic hit the iceberg?
4. Who saw the iceberg first?
5. Who got into the lifeboat first?
6. Why didn't Arthur Ryerson get into a lifeboat?

G. Listen and choose. Listen to each sentence. Circle the verb you hear.

1. The Titanic was carrying 2,224 passengers and crew.
2. All the passengers were enjoying their days aboard the luxury ship.
3. None of them knew of the danger ahead.
4. They were approaching icebergs.
5. Most passengers were sleeping.
6. Others were writing letters.
7. The band was finishing for the evening.
8. One of the crewmen was standing watch.
9. The iceberg ripped a 300-foot hole in the side.
10. They were still playing cards as the Titanic sank into the icy waters.

H. Listen and write. Listen to each sentence. Write the verb you hear.

1. All of the passengers were enjoying their trip.
2. The Titanic was carrying 2,224 passengers.
3. They were approaching icebergs.
4. Most passengers were getting ready for bed.
5. Other passengers were drinking.
6. The band was finishing for the evening.
7. Arthur Ryerson was playing cards.
8. One of the crewmen was standing watch.
9. The ship was filling with water.
10. The ship was sinking fast.

I. Listen and decide. You will hear a statement in the past continuous tense. Is the grammar correct or incorrect? Circle *correct* or *incorrect*.

1. The Titanic carrying 2,224 passengers.
2. All the passengers were enjoying their days aboard the ship.
3. They were approach icebergs.
4. Most passengers sleeping.
5. Other passengers were drink.

6. Arthur Ryerson playing cards.
7. One of the crewmen was standing watch.
8. The ship was fill with water.
9. It was sinking fast.
10. They were still playing cards as the Titanic sank into the icy waters.

21. Vicki

A. Fill in.   Listen to these sentences. Fill in the new words from the list above.
1. We have five senses: hearing, smelling, touch, taste, and sight.
2. Listening is not a sense; it's a skill. We must learn it.
3. A person who cannot hear well is called hearing impaired.
4. The results of the hearing test showed that Vicki was almost deaf.
5. A speech therapist is a teacher who helps people to learn to speak.
6. We wanted Vicki to learn to listen, we didn't want her to be dependent on speaking with her hands.
7. We didn't want Vicki to speak with her hands. We wanted a different approach.
8. The children played games to increase their listening skills.

STORY—UNIT 21—Vicki

Vicki was our first child. She was an active baby. She picked up her head, sat and walked at the same time as other children her age. She played and laughed. We waited for her to say her first words, but they didn't come.

We took Vicki for her first hearing and speech test when she was almost two years old. The results showed that Vicki was profoundly deaf. She could hear only very loud noises, like a motorcycle engine or an airplane. So, at two years of age, Vicki began to wear a body aid. This was like a hearing aid, only stronger.

We knew we had to begin early to help Vicki with her hearing and speech. We didn't want to wait until she began school. So we looked into several programs. In one school, the children learned signing; that is, how to talk with their hands. But we were worried that she would become too dependent on signing and not learn to listen or speak. We chose a different approach. We put Vicki in a special school for hearing impaired children. The school taught listening, speaking, and lip reading. The school believed that hearing is a sense; listening is a skill that must be learned. The children played games to increase their listening ability. In one game, each child took a box and a few blocks. Then the teacher told a story. Whenever the children heard a certain word, they dropped a block into the box. We worked with Vicki at home, too. We taught her the names of everything in the house. We did things with Vicki and carefully explained every action.

Vicki began to speak when she was three years old. At four, she was talking more, but we couldn't understand what she was saying. She started lessons with a speech therapist. The therapist developed her listening even more. Vicki listened, then followed directions with blocks, toys and other objects. The therapist described a picture. Vicki listened, then pointed to the part the therapist was describing. Vicki practiced her speaking, beginning with basic sounds, such as ba-ba-ba and ma-ma-ma.

When she was five, Vicki entered kindergarten in a regular public school. She's a second grader there now. Vicki is the only hearing impaired child in the school. In class, she wears an auditory trainer. This is a special hearing aid. The teacher wears a microphone on her clothes and Vicki carries the receiver in her pocket. Vicki hears only what the teacher says, not other noises, such as doors opening and closing and cars passing by. Vicki also works with a speech teacher one hour a day. Vicki is doing very well in school.

Vicki's speech is improving. Her sentences sometimes have the wrong verb tense or the words aren't in the correct order. We understand everything Vicki says, but at times other people ask her to repeat a word or sentence.

After school and speech lessons, it's time to get down to the business of being a normal seven year old. Vicki likes to play with her friends, ride her bicycle, and go to the park. She explains to friends that she is learning how to swim and can jump off the high dive. Vicki is proud of herself and we're proud of her, too.

F.   Comprehension questions.   Listen to each question. Circle the correct answer.
1. How old was Vicki when her parents learned that she was deaf?
2. What is signing?
3. Which approach did Vicki's parents choose?
4. How did Vicki's parents help her?
5. Why did the therapist ask Vicki to point to parts of the picture?
6. What kind of school does Vicki attend now?

G.   Listen and choose.   Listen to each sentence. Circle the verb you hear.
1. Vicki walked at the same time as other children her age.
2. We waited for her to say her first words.
3. In one school the children learned signing.
4. The children played listening games.
5. Vicki entered a regular kindergarten.
6. In school, Vicki wears an auditory trainer.
7. Vicki carries the receiver in her pocket.
8. Vicki is doing very well in school.
9. Her speech is improving.
10. Vicki likes to play with her friends.

H.   Listen and write.   Listen to each sentence. Write the verb you hear.
1. Vicki picked up her head at the same time as other children.
2. The results showed that Vicki was profoundly deaf.
3. We looked into several schools.
4. We chose a different approach.
5. The children dropped a block into the box.
6. Vicki's teacher wears a microphone.
7. Vicki only hears the teacher.
8. Vicki's speech is improving.
9. She works with a speech teacher one hour a day.
10. Vicki is learning how to swim.

22. Vi

A. Fill in.
Listen to these sentences. Fill in the new vocabulary words from the list above.
1. The ship was bound for the United States.
2. During the massacre, the soldiers killed all the residents of the town.
3. The students dug graves for the people who had been killed in the massacre.
4. When they heard that the soldiers were marching toward the city, the residents fled.
5. In the civil war, the North was fighting the South.
6. After he went to live with a friend, Vi felt more settled.
7. Vi's family escaped to Saigon. What were the alternatives after that?
8. Vi set high standards for his life.

STORY—UNIT 22—Vi

Vi talked on and on. "My life is a lot of pieces," he said, "like a puzzle. Some pieces fit together. I don't know where to put other ones."

Vi was born in DaNang, Vietnam in 1955. Vietnam is a country with a history of wars. In 1955, a civil war was taking place, with the North Vietnamese communists fighting the South. As a young child, Vi heard stories about the fighting in the North, but the war didn't affect his town or his family. As Vi became older, the fighting became more serious. The North Vietnamese communists attacked several towns in South Vietnam. Vi's family sent him away to high school to a safer area. But as the months went by, the students began to hear bombings and saw rockets in the sky. At times, he and other students gathered supplies for a bombed village. Once, there was a massacre in a nearby town. The students went to the town and helped dig graves for all who had been killed. The war was coming closer to home.

By 1974, the fighting was much more serious. The United States was fighting with the South Vietnamese against the North. But the South was losing. Towns in South Vietnam were falling to the North Vietnamese. Vi was now back home with his family. But DaNang was no longer safe. Vi and his family fled at night to the capital, Saigon, leaving their home, business, and belongings.

Vi and his family remained in Saigon for many months. They constantly discussed the alternatives. Should they go back to DaNang? Should they try to leave the country? Should they stay in Saigon? The North Vietnamese army was marching toward the capital. Vi, now twenty years old, decided to leave. His family stayed. At the United States embassy, Vi got in line with hundreds of other Vietnamese. A bus took him and many others to the airport. A helicopter flew them out of Vietnam and onto a waiting United States ship. Vi was now a political refugee, bound for the United States.

"My first year in the United States was crazy," comments Vi. "I was in Fort Chaffee in Arkansas, Oklahoma, then Texas. I had several different sponsors. I didn't know where I wanted to go or what I wanted to do." Vi had three different jobs. In the evenings, he studied English at different adult schools.

Finally, in 1977, a friend invited him to come to live in New Jersey. Vi accepted. His life became more settled and he decided to enter college. In order to attend, Vi held two part-time jobs and borrowed money from the government. In 1981, he graduated with a B.S. in industrial engineering. Vi states that he didn't have too much trouble with English in college. He adds that it was five times more difficult to understand the culture and feel comfortable with the people.

Vi now works as a design engineer for a consulting firm. He designs heating, ventilating and air conditioning systems. Vi is not satisfied with being "average." He says, "I wanted a job and standards that I would be satisfied with." Vi is still going to school. Sometimes he thinks of going to law school, other times he likes the idea of having his own engineering firm. Or, maybe he will teach. As he looks into the future, Vi hopes for a strong marriage, a good family, and a comfortable life in a small town.

F. Comprehension questions.
Listen to each question. Circle the correct answer.
1. Who was fighting in Vietnam in 1955?
2. What does this sentence mean, "The war was coming closer to home."
3. Why did Vi decide to leave Vietnam?
4. What did Vi do during his first year in this country?
5. How did Vi pay for college?
6. Which of these was the most difficult for Vi?

G. Listen and choose.
Listen to each sentence. Circle the verb you hear.
1. Some pieces fit together.
2. The fighting became more serious.
3. The students gathered supplies for a bombed village.
4. The South was losing.
5. Towns in South Vietnam were falling to the North Vietnamese.
6. Vi and his family remained in Saigon for many months.
7. Vi borrowed money from the government.
8. Vi works as a design engineer.
9. He thinks of going to law school.
10. He hopes for a strong marriage.

H. Listen and write.
Listen to each sentence. Write the verb you hear.
1. In 1955, a civil war was taking place.
2. The war was coming closer to home.
3. The United States was fighting along with the South Vietnamese.
4. Vi and his family fled at night to the capital.
5. In the evening he studied English.
6. Vi designs heating systems.
7. Vi is still going to school.
8. Maybe he will teach.
9. He hopes for a comfortable life in a small town.
10. Vi graduated with a B.S. in engineering.